The Britannica Guide to Islam

The Islamic World from 1041 to the Present

Edited by Ariana Wolff

Britannica Educational Publishing
in association with
Rosen Educational Services

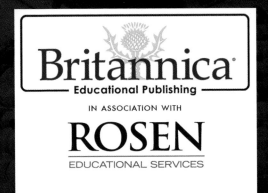

Published in 2018 by Britannica Educational Publishing (a trademark of Encyclopædia Britannica, Inc.) in association with The Rosen Publishing Group, Inc.
29 East 21st Street, New York, NY 10010

Distributed exclusively by Rosen Publishing.
To see additional Britannica Educational Publishing titles, go to rosenpublishing.com.

First Edition

Britannica Educational Publishing
J.E. Luebering: Director, Core Reference Group
Andrea R. Field: Managing Editor, Compton's by Britannica

Rosen Publishing
Ariana Wolff: Editor
Nelson Sá: Art Director
Brian Garvey: Series Designer
Tahara Anderson: Book Layout
Cindy Reiman: Photography Manager
Nicole diMella: Photo Researcher
Introduction and conclusion by Danielle Weiner.

Library of Congress Cataloging-in-Publication Data

Names: Wolff, Ariana, editor.
Title: The Islamic world from 1041 to the present / [editor] Ariana Wolff.
Description: New York, NY : Britannica Educational Publishing, 2018. |
Series: The Britannica guide to Islam | Includes bibliographical references and index.
Identifiers: LCCN 2016053707 | ISBN 9781680486179 (library bound : alk. paper)
Subjects: LCSH: Islamic countries—History. | Islamic civilization. | Islam—History.
Classification: LCC DS35.63 .I845 2018 | DDC 909/.09767—dc23
LC record available at https://lccn.loc.gov/2016053707

Manufactured in China

Photo credits: Cover, p. 1 ESB Professional/Shutterstock.com; pp. 7, 49 Encyclopædia Britannica, Inc.; p. 11 Darkydoors/Shutterstock.com; p. 13 Pictures from History/Bridgeman Images; p. 17 Iberfoto/SuperStock; p. 19 © Photos.com/Thinkstock; p. 22 Courtesy of the Edinburgh University Library, Scotland; p. 27 Courtesy of Istanbul University Library; p. 29 DEA Picture Library/Getty Images; p. 33 Guy Thouvenin/robertharding/SuperStock; p. 35 Heritage Images/Hulton Archive/Getty Images; p. 38 Nik Wheeler/Corbis Documentary/Getty Images; p. 40 Abraham Cresques/Getty Images; p. 45 DEA/A. Dagli Orti/De Agostini/Getty Images; p. 47 Tatiana Popova/Shutterstock.com; p. 53 Courtesy of the Smithsonian Institution, Freer Gallery of Art, Washington, D.C.; p. 55 Matjaz Krivic/Getty Images; p. 58 Courtesy of the India Office Library, London; p. 66 N. Cirani/De Agostini Picture Library/Getty Images; p. 72 Courtesy of the Victoria and Albert Museum, London; p. 76 Albert Harlingue/Roger Viollet/Getty Images; p. 78 Hulton Archive/Archive Photos/Getty Images; p. 84 AFP/Getty Images; p. 87 istanbul image video/Shutterstock.com; p. 89 Francois Lochon/Gamma-Rapho/Getty Images; p. 94 Orlok/Shutterstock.com; p. 96 Mahmoud Zayyat/AFP/Getty Images; p. 98 Marcel Mettelsiefen/picture-alliance/dpa/AP Images; p. 100 ©AP Images; p. 102 ZUMA Press Inc./Alamy Stock Photo; back cover, pp. 3-5 background design javarman/Shutterstock.com; interior pages border design Azat1976/shutterstock.com

CONTENTS

INTRODUCTION

There are 1.6 billion Muslims in the world today, making up 23 percent of the world's population and spread across diverse geographical locations. However, this was not always the case. A very broad perspective is required to explain the history of today's Islamic world. This approach must enlarge upon conventional political or dynastic divisions to draw a comprehensive picture of the stages by which successive Muslim communities, throughout Islam's 14 centuries, encountered and incorporated new peoples so as to produce an international religion and civilization.

Islamic history is a narrative of expansion and theological, political, cultural, and geographical transformation. Before 1041, the Islamic world had undergone two recognized periods of change. Instrumental in shaping Islamic theology and laying the groundwork for Islamic law, these are known as the "formative" and "classical" periods. In 1041, the Seljuq Turks defeated the Ghaznavid sultan in eastern Iran and allowed them to proclaim themselves rulers of Khorāsān, a region northeast of Persia. This would usher in Islamdom's second era of tribal expansion, the creation of societies in which Muslims and Islam were socially and politically dominant.

The period after 1041 saw the rise of Islamic courts and centres of access to Islamic culture in regions beyond Islam's previous geographical boundaries. This not only set the scene for Islam's expansion as a ruling system of law, but also produced theological changes. Differences between Sunnis, the majority sect of Islam today who believe that Abu Bakr was Muhammad's rightful successor, and Shīʿites, who believe Muhammad appointed his son-in-law Ali to be his successor, were solidified. The four schools of Islamic jurisprudence—*Hanafi, Shafii, Maliki,* and *Hanbali*, generally known as *madhabs*—arose at the end of the 11th century, providing a framework for theological and legalistic interpretation of Islam. The creation of state-supported schools of learning, *madrasas*, allowed Islam to be taught

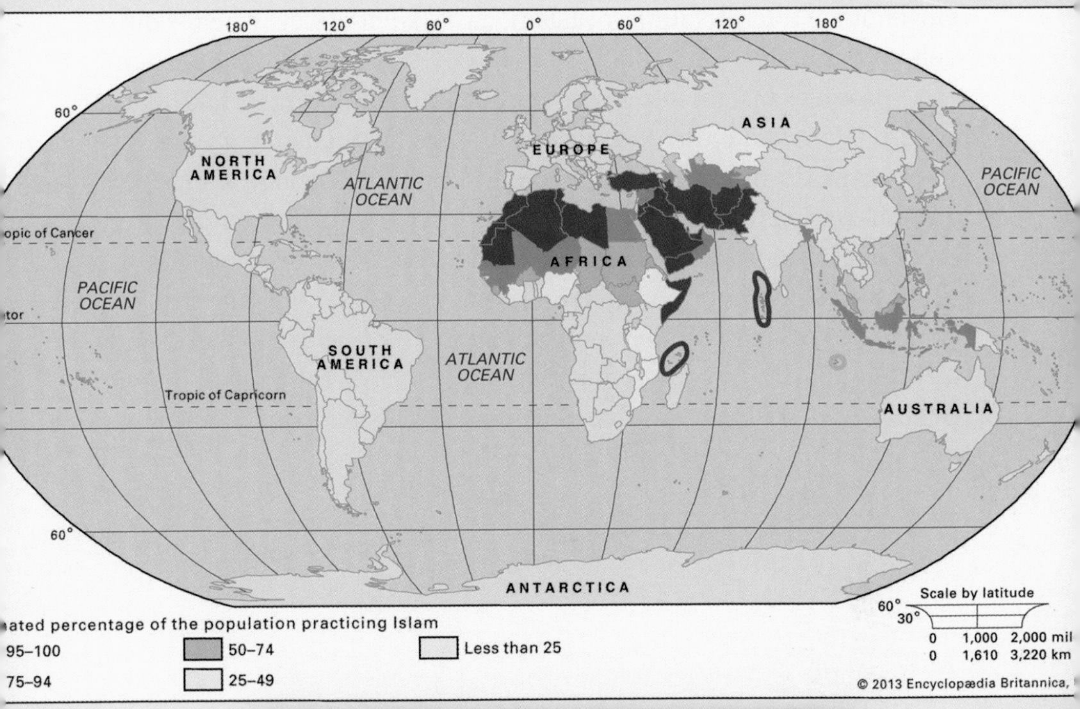

Map showing the estimated world distribution of Islam.

in localized regions. However, these *madrasas* would often serve as vehicles of political change and receptors of government stipends, constituting an infrastructure would again prove to be crucial in the facilitation of revival and regime in the late 20th century.

The changes in the Islamic world since the 11th century are concerned with political or dynastic divisions or clashes, and, later on, theological reform and revival. Such theological changes, including conservative, fundamentalist, imitative, adaptive, nationalist, and transnational interpretations of Islam, have larger effects when Islam is seen both as a religion and a system of law. The history of the Islamic world provides insight into structures that affect the current state both of modern Islam and of the Islamic world. Islam and Islamic governance are continually reformed and revived throughout history. Often, it is difficult to discern valid criticism of oppressive state interference from reactionary traditionalism. While religion forms the idiom and rhetoric of revolution and its criticism, it is clashes of a political nature that give rise to revolutionary action and violence. The history of the Islamic world demonstrates the complex entanglement of religious, political, geographical, and cultural divisions that spur growth and change, and from which no civilization is truly exempt.

Chapter 1

Migration and Renewal (1041–1405)

During this period, migrating peoples once again played a major role, perhaps greater than that of the Arabs during the 7th and 8th centuries. No other civilization in premodern history experienced so much in-migration, especially of alien and disruptive peoples, or showed a greater ability to assimilate as well as to learn from outsiders. Nowhere has the capacity of a culture to redefine and incorporate the strange and the foreign been more evident. In this period, which ends with the death in 1405 of Timur (Tamerlane), the last great tribal conqueror, the tense yet creative relationship between sedentary and migratory peoples emerged as one of the great themes of Islamicate history, played out as it was in the centre of the great arid zone of Eurasia. Because this period can be seen as the history of peoples as well as of regions, and because the mobility of those peoples brought them to more than one cultural region, this period should be treated group by group rather than region by region.

As a general term, "migrating" peoples is preferable because it does not imply aimlessness, as "nomadic" does; or herding, as "pastoralist" does; or kin-related, as "tribal" does. "Migrating" focuses simply on movement from one home to another. Although the Franks, as the Crusaders are called in Muslim sources, differed from other migrating peoples, most of whom were pastoralists related by kinship, they too were migrating warriors organized to invade and occupy peoples to whom they were hostile and alien. Though not literally tribal, they appeared to behave like a tribe with a distinctive way of life and a solidarity based on common values, language, and objectives. Viewing them as alien immigrants comparable to, say, the Mongols helps to explain their reception: how they came to be assimilated into the local culture and drawn into the intra-Muslim factional competition and fighting that was under way in Syria when they arrived.

TURKS

For almost 400 years a succession of Turkic peoples entered eastern Islamdom from Central Asia. These nearly continuous migrations can be divided into three phases: Seljuqs (1055–92), Mongols (1256–1411), and neo-Mongols (1369–1405). Their long-term impact, more constructive than destructive on balance, can still be felt through the lingering heritage of the great Muslim empires they inspired. The addition of tribally organized warrior Turks to the already widely used Turkic slave soldiery gave a single ethnic group an extensive role in widening the gap between rulers and ruled.

SELJUQ TURKS

The Seljuqs were a family among the Oghuz Turks, a label applied to the migratory pastoralists of the Syr Darya–Oxus basin. Their name has come to stand for the group of Oghuz families led into Ghaznavid Khorāsān after they had been converted to Sunni Islam, probably by Sufi missionaries after the beginning of the 11th century. In 1040 the Seljuqs' defeat of the Ghaznavid sultan allowed them to proclaim themselves rulers of Khorāsān. Having expanded into western Iran as well, Toghrïl Beg, also using the title "sultan," was able to occupy Baghdad (1055) after "petitioning" the ʿAbbāsid caliph for permission. The Seljuqs quickly took the remaining Būyid territory and began to occupy Syria, whereupon they encountered Byzantine resistance in the Armenian highlands. In 1071 a Seljuq army under Alp-Arslan defeated the Byzantines at Manzikert north of Lake Van; while the main Seljuq army replaced the Fāṭimids in Syria, large independent tribal bands occupied Anatolia, coming closer to the Byzantine capital than had any other Muslim force.

A statue of Seljuq, the eponymous hero of the Seljuq Turks, who, in the 11th century CE, rose to power and became the leading Muslim dynasty of the era.

Policies of Niẓām al-Mulk

The Seljuqs derived their legitimacy from investiture by the caliph, and from "helping" him reunite the *ummah* (Muslim community); yet their governing style prefigured the emergence of true alternatives to the caliphate. Some of their Iranian advisers urged them to restore centralized absolutism as it had existed in pre-Islamic times and in the period of Marwānid-ʿAbbāsid strength. The best-known proponent was Niẓām al-Mulk, chief minister to the second and third Seljuq sultans, Alp-Arslan and Malik-Shāh. Niẓām al-Mulk explained his plans in his *Seyāsat-nāmeh* (*The Book of Government*), one of the best-known manuals of Islamicate political theory and administration. He was unable, however, to persuade the Seljuq sultans to assert enough power over other tribal leaders. Eventually the Seljuq sultans, like so many rulers before them, alienated their tribal supporters and resorted to the costly alternative of a Turkic slave core, whose leading members were appointed to tutor and train young princes of the Seljuq family to compete for rule on the death of the reigning sultan. The tutors were known as *atabegs*; more often than not, they became the actual rulers of the domains assigned to their young charges, cooperating with urban notables (*aʿyān*) in day-to-day administration.

Although Niẓām al-Mulk was not immediately successful, he did contribute to long-term change. He encouraged the establishment of state-supported schools (*madrasas*); those he personally patronized were called Niẓāmiyyahs. The most important Niẓāmiyyah was founded in Baghdad in 1067; there Niẓām al-Mulk gave government stipends to teachers and students whom he hoped he could subsequently not only appoint to the position of *qāḍī* but also recruit for the bureaucracy. Systematic and broad instruction in Jamāʿī-Sunni learning would counteract the disruptive influences of non-Sunni or anti-Sunni thought and activity, particularly the continuing agitation of Ismāʿīlī Muslims. In 1090 a group of Ismāʿīlīs established themselves in a mountain fortress at Alamūt in the mountains of Daylam. From there they began to coordinate revolts all over Seljuq domains. Nominally loyal to the Fāṭimid caliph in Cairo, the eastern Ismāʿīlīs confirmed their growing independence and radicalism by supporting a failed contender for the

As chief minister to the second and third Seljuq sultans, Niẓām al-Mulk encouraged the establishment of *madrasas*, or state-supported centres of learning.

Fāṭimid caliphate, Nizār. For that act they were known as the Nizārī Ismāʿīlīs. They were led by Ḥasan-e Ṣabbāḥ and were dubbed by their detractors the *ḥashīshiyyīn* (assassins) because they practiced political murder while they were allegedly under the influence of hashish.

Niẓām al-Mulk's *madrasa* system enhanced the prestige and solidarity of the Jamāʿī-Sunni ulama without actually drawing them into the bureaucracy or combating anti-Sunni agitation, but it also undermined their autonomy. It established the connection between state-supported education and office holding, and it subordinated the spiritual power and prestige of the ulama to the indispensable physical force of the military emirs. Niẓām al-Mulk unintentionally encouraged the independence of these emirs by extending the *iqṭā*ʿ system beyond Būyid practice; he regularly assigned land revenues to individual military officers, assuming that he could keep them under bureaucratic control. When that failed, his system increased the emirs' independence and drained the central treasury.

The *madrasa* system had other unpredictable results that can be illustrated by al-Ghazālī, who was born in 1058 at Ṭūs and in 1091 was made head of the Baghdad Niẓāmiyyah. For four years, to great admiration, he taught both *fiqh* and *kalām* and delivered critiques of falsafah and Ismāʿīlī thought. According to his autobiographical work *Al-Munqidh min al-ḍalāl* (*The Deliverer from Error*), the more he taught, the more he doubted, until his will and voice became paralyzed. In 1095 he retreated from public life, attempting to arrive at a more satisfying faith. He undertook a radically skeptical reexamination of all of the paths available to the pious Muslim, culminating in an incorporation of the active, immediate, and inspired experience of the Sufis into the Sharīʿah-ordered piety of the public cult. For his accomplishments, al-Ghazālī was viewed as a renewer (*mujaddid*), a role expected by many Muslims to be filled by at least one figure at the turn of every Muslim century.

Ṭarīqah Fellowships

In the 12th century Muslims began to group themselves into *ṭarīqah*, fellowships organized around and named for the *ṭarīqah* ("way" or "path") of given masters. Al-Ghazālī may have had such a following himself. One of the first large-scale orders, the Qādirīyah, formed around the teachings of ʿAbd al-Qādir al-Jīlānī of Baghdad. Though rarely monastic in the European sense, the activities of a *ṭarīqah* often centred around assembly halls (called *khānqāh, zāwiyah*, or *tekke*) that could serve as places of retreat or accommodate special spiritual exercises. The *dhikr*, for example, is a ceremony in which devotees meditated on the name of God to the accompaniment of breathing exercises, music, or movement, so as to attain a state of consciousness productive of a sense of union with God. Although shortcuts and excesses have often made Sufism vulnerable to criticism, its most serious practitioners have conceived of it as a disciplined extension of Sharīʿah-minded piety, not an escape. In fact, many Sufis have begun their path through fulfillment of standard ritual requirements.

Thousands of *ṭarīqahs* sprang up over the centuries, some associated with particular occupations, locales, or classes. It is possible that by the 18th century most adult Muslim males had some connection with one or more *ṭarīqahs*. The structure of the *ṭarīqah* ensued from the charismatic authority of the master, who, though not a prophet, replicated the direct intimacy that the prophets had shared with God. This quality he passed on to his disciples through a hierarchically ordered network that could extend over thousands of miles. The *ṭarīqahs* thus became powerful centripetal forces among societies in which formal organizations were rare; but the role of the master became controversial because followers often made saints or intercessors of especially powerful Sufi leaders and made shrines or pilgrimage sites of their tombs or birthplaces. Long before these developments could combine to produce stable alternatives to the caliphal system, Seljuq power had begun to decline, only to be replaced for a century and a half with a plethora of small military states. When the Frankish Crusaders arrived in the Holy Land in 1099, no one could prevent them from quickly establishing themselves along the eastern Mediterranean coast.

FRANKS

At the Council of Clermont in 1095 Pope Urban II responded to an appeal from the Byzantine emperor for help against the Seljuq Turks, who had expanded into western Anatolia just as the Kipchak Turks in the Ukraine had cut off newly Christian Russia from Byzantium. The First Crusade, begun the next year, brought about the conquest of Jerusalem in 1099. The Christian Reconquista (Reconquest) of Spain was already under way, having scored its first great victory at Toledo in 1085. Ironically, modern historiography has concentrated on the Crusades that failed and virtually ignored the ones that succeeded. In the four centuries between the fall of Toledo and the fall of Granada (1492), Spanish Christians replaced Muslim rulers throughout the Iberian Peninsula, although Muslims remained as a minority under Christian rule until the early 17th century. In the 200 years from the fall of Jerusalem to the end of the Eighth Crusade (1291), western European Crusaders failed to halt the Turkish advance or to establish a permanent presence in the Holy Land. By 1187 local Muslims had managed to retake Jerusalem and thereby contain Christian ambitions permanently. By the time of the Fourth Crusade (1202–04) the Crusading movement had been turned inward against Christian heretics such as the Byzantines.

***The Surrender of Granada*, oil on canvas by Francisco Pradilla Ortiz, 1882.**

The direct impact of the Crusades on Islamdom was limited largely to Syria. For the century during which western European Christians were a serious presence there, they were confined to their massive coastal fortifications. The Crusaders had arrived in Syria at one of its most factionalized periods prior to the 20th century. Seljuq control, never strong, was then insignificant; local Muslim rule was anarchic; the Seljuq regime in Baghdad was competing with the Fāṭimid regime in Egypt; and all parties in Syria were the target of the Nizārī Ismāʿīlī movement at Alamūt. The Crusaders soon found it difficult to operate as more than just another faction. Yet the significance of the Crusaders as a force against which to be rallied should not be underestimated any more than should the significance of Islamdom as a force against which Christendom could unite.

The Crusaders' situation encouraged interaction with the local population and even assimilation. They needed the food, supplies, and services available in the Muslim towns. Like their Christian counterparts in Spain, they took advantage of the enemy's superior skills in medicine and hygiene, for example. Because warfare was seasonal and occasional, they spent much of their time in peaceful interaction with their non-Christian counterparts. Some early-generation Crusaders intermarried with Arab Muslims or Arab Christians and adopted their personal habits and tastes, much to the dismay of Christian latecomers. An intriguing account of life in Syria during the Crusades can be found in the *Kitāb al-Iʿtibār* ("Book of Reflection"), the memoirs of Usāmah ibn Munqidh (1095–1188). Born in Syria, he was a small boy when the first generation of Franks controlled Jerusalem. As an adult, he fought with Saladin (Ṣalāḥ al-Dīn Yūsuf ibn Ayyūb) and lived to see him unite Egypt with Syria and restore Jerusalem to Muslim control. In this fine example of Islamicate autobiographical writing, Usāmah draws a picture of the Crusades not easily found in European sources: Christians and Muslims observing, and sometimes admiring, each others' skills and habits, from the battlefield to the bathhouse. Although the Franks in Syria were clearly influenced by the Muslims, the Crusades seem to have contributed relatively little to the overall impact of Islamicate culture on Europe, even though they constituted the most prolonged direct contact.

Although the Crusaders never formed a united front against the Muslims, Syrian Muslims did eventually form a united front against them, largely through the efforts of the family of the emir Zangī, a Turkic slave officer appointed Seljuq representative in Mosul in 1127. After Zangī had extended his control through northern Syria, one of his sons and successors, Nūr al-Dīn (Nureddin), based at Aleppo, was able to tie Zangī's movement to the frontier warrior (*ghāzī*) spirit. This he used to draw together urban and military support for a jihad against

Siege of Acre (1191) during the Third Crusade, illustration from the 13th-century encyclopaedia *Speculum majus* ("Great Mirror").

the Christians. After taking Damascus, he established a second base in Egypt. He offered help to the failing Fāṭimid regime in return for being allowed to place one of his own lieutenants, Saladin, as chief minister to the Fāṭimid caliph, thus warding off a Crusader alliance with the Fāṭimids. This action gave Nūr al-Dīn two fronts from which to counteract the superior seaborne and naval support the Crusaders were receiving from western Europe and the Italian city-states. Three years before Nūr al-Dīn's death in 1174, Saladin substituted himself for the Fāṭimid caliph he theoretically served, thus ending more than 200 years of Fāṭimid rule in Egypt. When Nūr al-Dīn died, Saladin succeeded him as head of the whole movement. When Saladin died in 1193, he had recaptured Jerusalem (1187) and begun the reunification of Egypt and Syria; his successors were known, after his patronymic, as the Ayyūbids. The efforts of a contemporary ʿAbbāsid caliph, al-Nāṣir, to revive the caliphate seem pale by comparison.

The Ayyūbids ruled in Egypt and Syria until around 1250, when they were replaced first in Egypt and later in Syria by the leaders of their own slave-soldier corps, the Mamlūks. It was they who expelled the remaining Crusaders from Syria, subdued the remaining Nizārī Ismāʿīlīs there, and consolidated Ayyūbid holdings into a centralized state. That state became strong enough in its first decade to do what no other Muslim power could: in 1260 at ʿAyn Jālūt, south of Damascus, the Mamlūk army defeated the recently arrived Mongols and expelled them from Syria.

MONGOLS

The Mongols were pagan, horse-riding tribes of the northeastern steppes of Central Asia. In the early 13th century, under the leadership of Genghis Khan, they formed, led, and gave their name to a confederation of Turkic tribes that they channeled into a movement of global expansion, spreading east into China, north into Russia, and west into Islamdom. Like other migratory peoples before them, Arabs, Imazighen, and Turks, they had come to be involved in citied life through their role in the caravan trade. Unlike others, however, they did not convert to Islam before their arrival. Furthermore, they brought a greater hostility to sedentary civilization, a more ferocious military force, a more cumbersome material culture, a more complicated and hierarchical social structure, and a more coherent sense of tribal law. Their initial impact was physically more destructive than that of previous invaders, and their long-term impact perhaps more socially and politically creative.

FIRST MONGOL INCURSIONS

The first Mongol incursions into Islamdom in 1220 were a response to a challenge from the Khwārezm-Shāh ʿAlāʾ al-Dīn Muḥammad, the aggressive reigning leader of a dynasty formed in the Oxus Delta by a local governor who had rebelled against the Seljuq regime in Khorāsān. Under Genghis Khan's leadership, Mongol forces destroyed numerous cities in Transoxania and Khorāsān in an unprecedented display of terror and annihilation. By the time of Genghis Khan's death in 1227, his empire stretched from the Caspian Sea to the Sea of Japan. A later successor, Möngke, decided to extend the empire in two new directions. From the Mongol capital of Karakorum, he simultaneously dispatched Kublai Khan to southern China (where Islam subsequently began to expand inland) and Hülegü to Iran (1256). Hülegü had already received Sunni ambassadors who encouraged him to destroy the Ismāʿīlī state at Alamūt; this he did and more, reaching Baghdad in 1258, where he terminated and replaced the caliphate. The ʿAbbāsid line continued,

This miniature painting of Mongol warriors was created for an Islamic history book, Rashīd al-Dīn's *History of the World* of 1307.

however, until 1517; the Mamlūk sultan Baybars I, shortly after his defeat of the Mongols, invited a member of the ʿAbbāsid house to "invest" him and to live in Cairo as spiritual head of all Muslims.

The Mongol regimes in Islamdom quickly became rivals. The Il-Khans controlled the Tigris-Euphrates valley and Iran; the Chagatai dominated the Syr Darya and Oxus basins, the Kābul mountains, and eventually the Punjab; and the Golden Horde was concentrated in the Volga basin. The Il-Khans ruled in the territories where Islam was most firmly established. They patronized learning of all types and scholars from all parts of the vast Mongol empire, especially China. Demonstrating a special interest in nature, they built a major observatory at Marāgheh. Just as enthusiastically as they had destroyed citied life, they now rebuilt it, relying as had all previous invaders of Iran on the administrative skills of indigenous Persian-speaking bureaucrats.

The writings of one of these men, ʿAṭā Malek Joveynī, who was appointed governor in Baghdad after the Mongol capture of that city in 1258, described the type of rule the Mongols sought to impose. It has been called the military patronage state because it involved a reciprocal relationship between the foreign tribal military conquerors and their subjects. The entire state was defined as a single mobile military force connected to the household of the monarch; with no fixed capital, it moved with the monarch. All non-Turkic state workers, bureaucratic or religious, even though not military specialists, were defined as part of the army (*asker*); the rest of the subject population, as the herds (*raʿiyyah*). The leading tribal families could dispose of the wealth of the conquered populations as they wished, except that their natural superiority obligated them to reciprocate by patronizing whatever of excellence the cities could produce. What the Ghaznavids and Seljuqs had begun, the Mongols now accomplished. The self-confidence and superiority of the leading families were bolstered by a fairly elaborate set of tribal laws, inherited from Genghis Khan and known as the Yasa, which served to regulate personal status and criminal liability among the Mongol elite, as did the Sharīʿah among Muslims. In Il-Khanid hands, this dynastic law merely coexisted but did not compete with Sharīʿah; but in later Turkic regimes a reconciliation was achieved that extended the power of the rulers beyond the limitations of an autonomous Sharīʿah.

Conversion of Mongols to Islam

For a time the Il-Khans tolerated and patronized all religious persuasions—Sunni, Shīʿite, Buddhist, Nestorian Christian, Jewish, and pagan. But in 1295 a Buddhist named Maḥmūd Ghāzān became khan and declared himself Muslim, compelling other Mongol notables to follow suit. His patronage of Islamicate learning fostered such brilliant writers as Rashīd al-Dīn, the physician and scholar who authored one of the most famous Persian universal histories of all time. The Mongols, like other Islamicate dynasties swept into power by a tribal confederation, were able to unify their domains for only a few generations. By the 1330s their rule had begun to be fragmented among myriad local leaders. Meanwhile, on both Mongol flanks, other Turkic Muslim powers were increasing in strength.

To the east the Delhi Sultanate of Turkic slave-soldiers withstood Mongol pressure, benefited from the presence of scholars and administrators fleeing Mongol destruction, and gradually began to extend Muslim control south into India, a feat that was virtually accomplished under Muḥammad ibn Tughluq. Muslim Delhi was a culturally lively place that attracted a variety of unusual persons. Muḥammad ibn Tughluq himself was, like many later Indian Muslim rulers, well-read in philosophy, science, and religion. Not possessing the kind of dynastic legitimacy the pastoralist Mongols had asserted, he tied his legitimacy to his support for the Sharīʿah, and he even sought to have himself invested by the ʿAbbāsid "caliph" whom the Mamlūks had taken to Cairo. His concern with the Sharīʿah coincided with the growing popularity of Sufism, especially as represented by the massive Chishti *ṭarīqah*. Its most famous leader, Niẓām al-Dīn Awliyāʾ, had been a spiritual adviser to many figures at court before Muḥammad ibn Tughluq came to the throne, as well as to individual

Hindus and Muslims alike. In India, Sufism, which inherently undermined communalism, was bringing members of different religious communities together in ways very rare in the more westerly parts of Islamdom.

To the west the similarly constituted Mamlūk state continued to resist Mongol expansion. Its sultans were chosen on a nonhereditary basis from among a group of freed slaves who acted as the leaders of the various slave corps. At the death of one sultan, the various military corps would compete to see whose leader would become the next sultan. The leaders of the various slave corps formed an oligarchy that exercised control over the sultan. Although political instability was the frequent and natural result of such a system, cultural florescence did occur. The sultans actively encouraged trade and building, and Mamlūk Cairo became a place of splendour, filled with numerous architectural monuments. While the Persian language was becoming the language of administration and high culture over much of Islamdom, Arabic alone continued to be cultivated in Mamlūk domains, to the benefit of a diversified intellectual life. Ibn al-Nafīs (died 1288), a physician, wrote about pulmonary circulation 300 years before it was "discovered" in Europe. For Mamlūk administrative personnel, al-Qalqashandī composed an encyclopaedia in which he surveyed not only local practice but also all the information that a cultivated administrator should know. Ibn Khallikān composed one of the most important Islamicate biographical works, a dictionary of eminent men. Sharīʿah-minded studies were elaborated: the ulama worked out a political theory that tried to make sense of the sultanate, and they also explored the possibility of enlarging on the Sharīʿah by reference to *falsafah* and Sufism.

However, in much the same way as al-Shāfiʿī had responded in the 9th century to what he viewed as dangerous legal diversity, another great legal and religious reformer, Ibn Taymiyyah, living in Mamlūk

Damascus in the late 13th and early 14th century, cautioned against such extralegal practices and pursuits. He insisted that the Sharīʿah was complete in and of itself and could be adapted to every age by any *faqīh* who could analogize according to the principle of human advantage (*maṣlaḥah*). A Ḥanbalī himself, Ibn Taymiyyah became as popular as his school's founder, Aḥmad ibn Ḥanbal. Like him, Ibn Taymiyyah attacked all practices that undermined what he felt to be the fundamentals of Islam, including all forms of Shīʿite thought as well as aspects of Jamāʿī-Sunni piety (often influenced by the Sufis) that stressed knowledge of God over service to him. Most visible among such practices was the revering of saints' tombs, which was condoned by the Mamlūk authorities. Ibn Taymiyyah's program and popularity so threatened the Mamlūk authorities that they put him in prison, where he died. His movement did not survive, but when his ideas surfaced in the revolutionary movement of the Wahhābiyyah in the late 18th century, their lingering power became dramatically evident.

Farther west, the Rūm Seljuqs at Konya submitted to the Mongols in 1243 but survived intact. They continued to cultivate the Islamicate arts, architecture in particular. The most famous Muslim ever to live at Konya, Jalāl al-Dīn Rūmī, had emigrated from eastern Iran with his father before the arrival of the Mongols. In Konya, Jalāl al-Dīn, attracted to Sufi activities, attached himself to the master Shams al-Dīn. The poetry inspired by Jalāl al-Dīn's association with Shams al-Dīn is unparalleled in Persian literature. Its recitation, along with music and movement, was a key element in the devotional activities of Jalāl al-Dīn's followers, who came to be organized into a Sufi *ṭarīqah*—named the Mevleviyah (Mawlawiyyah) after their title of respect for him, Mevlana ("Our Master"). In his poetry Jalāl al-Dīn explored all varieties of metaphors, including intoxication, to describe the ineffable ecstasy of union with God.

ASCENT OF THE OTTOMAN TURKS

It was not from the Rūm Seljuqs, however, that lasting Muslim power in Anatolia was to come, but rather from one of the warrior states on the Byzantine frontier. The successive waves of Turkic migrations had driven unrelated individuals and groups across central Islamdom into Anatolia. Avoiding the Konya state, they gravitated toward an open frontier to the west, where they began to constitute themselves, often through fictitious kinship relationships, into quasi-tribal states that depended on raiding each other and Byzantine territory and shipping. One of these, the Osmanlıs, or Ottomans, named for their founder, Osman I (ruled 1281–1324), was located not on the coast, where raiding had its limits, but in Bithynia just facing Constantinople. In the mid-1320s they won the town of Bursa and made it their first capital. From Anatolia they crossed over into Thrace in the service of rival factions at Constantinople, then began to occupy Byzantine territory,

Osman I, miniature from a 16th-century manuscript illustrating the dynasty; in Istanbul University Library (Ms. Yildiz 2653/261).

establishing their second capital at Edirne on the European side. Their sense of legitimacy was complex. They were militantly Muslim, bound by the *ghāzī* spirit, spurred on in their intolerance of local Christians by Greek converts and traveling Sufis who gravitated to their domains. At the same time, ulama from more-settled Islamic lands to the east encouraged them to abide by the Sharīʿah and tolerate the Christians as protected non-Muslims. The Ottomans also cast themselves as deputies of the Rūm Seljuqs, who were themselves originally "deputized" by the ʿAbbāsid caliph. Finally they claimed descent from the leading Oghuz Turk families, who were natural rulers over sedentary populations. Under Murad I (ruled *c.* 1360–89) the state began to downplay its warrior fervour in favour of more conventional Islamicate administration.

Instead of relying on volunteer warriors, Murad established a regular cavalry, which he supported with land assignments, as well as a specially trained infantry force called the "New Troops," Janissaries, drawn from converted captives. Expanding first through western Anatolia and Thrace, the Ottomans under Bayezid I (ruled 1389–1402) turned their eyes toward eastern and southern Anatolia; just as they had incorporated the whole, they encountered a neo-Mongol conqueror expanding into Anatolia from the east who utterly defeated their entire army in a single campaign (1402).

TIMUR'S EFFORTS TO RESTORE MONGOL POWER

Timur (Tamerlane) was a Turk, not a Mongol, but he aimed to restore Mongol power. He was born a Muslim in the Syr Darya valley and served local pagan Mongol warriors and finally the Chagatai heir apparent, but he rebelled and made himself ruler in Khwārezm in 1380. He planned to restore Mongol supremacy under a thoroughly Islamic program. He surpassed the Mongols in terror, constructing

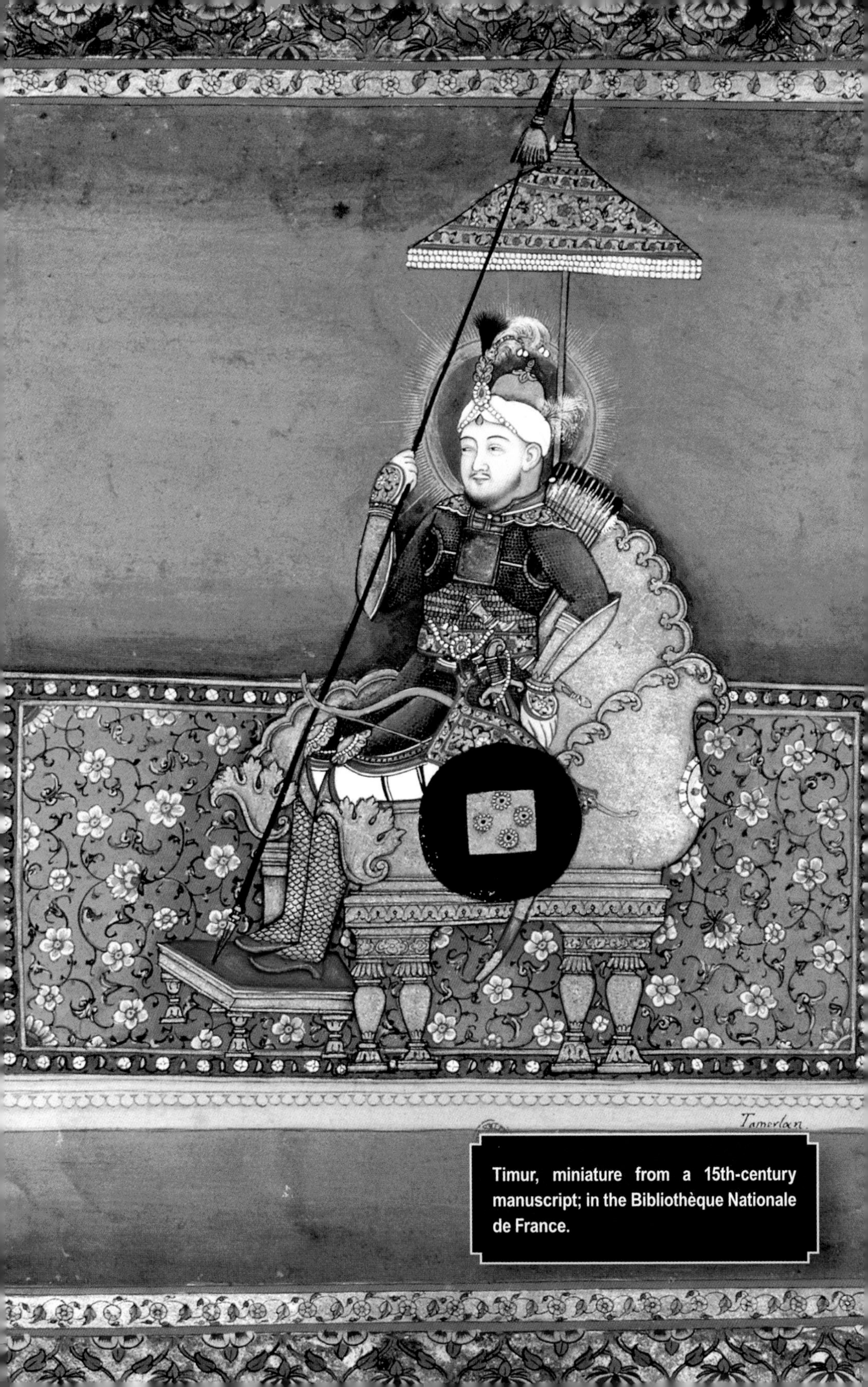

Timur, miniature from a 15th-century manuscript; in the Bibliothèque Nationale de France.

towers out of the heads of his victims. Having established himself in Iran, he moved first on India and then on Ottoman Anatolia and Mamlūk Syria, but he died before he could consolidate his realm. His impact was twofold: his defeat of the Ottomans inspired a comeback that would produce one of the greatest Islamicate empires of all time, and one of the Central Asian heirs to his tradition of conquest would found another great Islamicate empire in India. These later empires managed to find the combination of Turkic and Islamic legitimacy that could produce the stable centralized absolutism that had eluded all previous Turkic conquerors.

Arabs

When the Fāṭimids conquered Egypt in 969, they left a governor named Zīrī in the Maghrib (a region of North Africa bordering the

The Maghrib

The Maghrib (in Arabic, "West") is a region of North Africa bordering the Mediterranean Sea. The Africa Minor of the ancients, it at one time included Moorish Spain and now comprises essentially the Atlas Mountains and the coastal plain of Morocco, Algeria, Tunisia, and Libya. The weather of the Maghrib is characterized by prevailing westerly winds, which drop most of their moisture on the northern slopes and coastal plain, leaving little for the southern slopes, which maintain desert scrub fading into true desert in the Sahara to the south.

From the vastness of their mountain ranges, the native peoples of the Maghrib have resisted successive Punic, Roman, and Christian invasions. Not until the 7th and 8th centuries was the Maghrib conquered; the Arabs, who imposed on the native peoples the religion of Islam and Arabic, the language of the Qu'rān, thus absorbed the Maghrib into the Muslim civilization. Despite this absorption, most of the North African societies have preserved their cultural identity throughout the centuries.

The people of the Maghrib belong to both Berber and Arab ethnolinguistic groups. The Berbers are descended from the earlier inhabitants of the region and may trace their ancestry to Paleolithic times. Many other groups have invaded the area, including the Phoenicians, the Arabs, and the French. About one-sixth of the population of the Maghrib still speak one of the Berber languages (most of them in Algeria and Morocco), but most also speak some form of Arabic.

Mediterranean Sea). In the 1040s the dynasty founded by Zīrī declared its independence from the Fāṭimids, but it too was challenged by breakaways such as the Zanātah in Morocco and the Ḥammādids in Algeria. Gradually the Zīrids were restricted to the eastern Maghrib. There they were invaded from Egypt by two Bedouin Arab tribes, the Banū Halīl and the Banū Sulaym, at the instigation (1052) of the Fāṭimid ruler in Cairo. This mass migration of warriors as well as wives and children is known as the Hilālian invasion. Though initially disruptive, the Hilālian invasion had an important cultural impact: it resulted in a much greater spread of the Arabic language than had occurred in the 7th century and inaugurated the real Arabization of the Maghrib.

IMAZIGHEN

When the Arab conquerors arrived in the Maghrib in the 7th century, the indigenous peoples they met were the Imazighen (Berbers; singular Amazigh), a group of predominantly but not entirely migratory tribes who spoke a recognizably common Afro-Asiatic language with significant dialectal variations. Amazigh tribes could be found from present-day Morocco to present-day Algeria and from the Mediterranean to the Sahara. As among the Arabs, small tribal groupings of Imazighen occasionally formed short-lived confederations or became involved in caravan trade. No previous conqueror had tried to assimilate the Imazighen, but the Arabs quickly converted them and enlisted their aid in further conquests. Without their help, for example, Andalusia could never have been incorporated into the Islamicate state. At first only Imazighen nearer the coast were involved, but by the 11th century Muslim affiliation had begun to spread far into the Sahara.

The Ṣanhājah Confederation

One particular western Saharan Amazigh confederation, the Ṣanhājah, was responsible for the first Amazigh-directed effort to control the Maghrib. The Ṣanhājah were camel herders who traded mined salt for gold with the black kingdoms of the south. By the 11th century their power in the western Sahara was being threatened by expansion both from other Amazigh tribes, centred at Sijilmassa, and from the Soninke state at Ghana to the south, which had actually captured their capital of Audaghost in 990. The subsequent revival of their fortunes parallels Muḥammad's revitalization of the Arabs 500 years earlier, in that Muslim ideology reinforced their efforts to unify several smaller groups. The Ṣanhājah had been in contact with Islam since the 9th century, but their distance from major centres of Muslim life had kept their knowledge of the faith minimal.

In 1035, however, Yaḥyā ibn Ibrāhīm, a chief from one of their tribes, the Gudālah, went on hajj. For the Maghribi pilgrim, the cultural impact of the hajj was experienced not only in Mecca and Medina but also on the many stops along the 3,000-mile overland route. When Yaḥyā returned, he was accompanied by a teacher from Nafis (in present-day Libya), ʿAbd Allāh ibn Yāsīn, who would instruct the Imazighen in Islam as teachers under ʿUmar I had instructed the Arab fighters in the first Muslim garrisons. Having met with little initial success, the two are said to have retired to a *ribāṭ*, a fortified place of seclusion, perhaps as far south as an island in the Sénégal River, to pursue a purer religious life. The followers they attracted to that *ribāṭ* were known, by derivation, as *al-murābiṭūn* (Arabic: "those who are garrisoned"); the dynasty they founded came to be known by the same name, or Almoravids in its Anglicized form. In 1042 Ibn Yāsīn declared a jihad against the Ṣanhājah tribes, including his own, as people who had embraced Islam but then failed to practice it properly. By his death in 1059, the Ṣanhājah confederation had been restored

An Almoravid domed structure stands in Marrakech, Morocco.

under an Islamic ideology, and the conquest of Morocco, which lacked strong leadership, was under way.

The Almoravid Dynasty

Ibn Yāsīn's spiritual role was taken by a consultative body of ulama. His successor as military commander was Abū Bakr ibn ʿUmar. While pursuing the campaign against Morocco, Abū Bakr had to go south, leaving his cousin Yūsuf ibn Tāshufīn as his deputy. When Abū Bakr tried to return, Ibn Tāshufīn turned him back to the south, where he remained until his death in 1087. Under Ibn Tāshufīn's leadership, by 1082, Almoravid control extended as far as Algiers. In 1086 Ibn Tāshufīn responded to a request for help from the Andalusian party kings, unable to defend themselves against the Christian kingdoms in the north, such as Castile. By 1110 all Muslim states in Andalusia had come under Almoravid control.

Like most other Jamāʿī-Sunni rulers of his time, Ibn Tāshufīn had himself "appointed" deputy by the caliph in Baghdad. He also based his authority on the claim to bring correct Islam to peoples who had strayed from it. For him, "correct" Islam meant the Sharīʿah as developed by the Mālikī *faqīhs*, who played a key role in the Almoravid state by working out the application of the Sharīʿah to everyday problems. Like their contemporaries elsewhere, they received stipends from the government, sat in the ruler's council, went on campaign with him, and gave him recommendations (fatwas) on important decisions. This was an approach to Islam far more current than the one it had replaced but still out of touch with the liveliest intellectual developments. During the next phase of Amazigh activism, newer trends from the east reached the Maghrib.

A second major Amazigh movement originated in a revolt begun against Almoravid rule in 1125 by Ibn Tūmart, a settled

Maṣmūdah Amazigh from the Atlas Mountains. Like Ibn Yāsīn, Ibn Tūmart had been inspired by the hajj, which he used as an opportunity to study in Baghdad, Cairo, and Jerusalem, acquainting himself with all current schools of Islamic thought and becoming a disciple of the ideas of the recently deceased al-Ghazālī. Emulating his social activism, Ibn Tūmart was inspired to act on the familiar Muslim dictum, "Command the good and forbid the reprehensible." His early attempts took two forms, disputations with the scholars of the Almoravid court and public chastisement of Muslims who in his view contradicted the rules of Islam; he went so far as to throw the Almoravid ruler's sister off her horse because she was unveiled in public. His activities aroused hostility, and he fled to the safety of his own people. There, like Muhammad, he grew from teacher of a personal following to leader of a social movement.

Like many subsequent reformers, especially in Africa and other outlying Muslim lands, Ibn Tūmart used Muhammad's career

The Tinmel Mosque in the High Atlas mountains was built in 1158 in commemoration of Ibn Tūmart, founder of the Almohad Dynasty.

as a model. He interpreted the Prophet's rejection and retreat as an emigration (*hijrah*) that enabled him to build a community, and he divided his followers into *muhājirūn* ("fellow emigrants") and *anṣār* ("helpers"). He preached the idea of surrender to God to a people who had strayed from it. Thus could Muhammad's ability to bring about radical change through renewal be invoked without actually claiming the prophethood that he had sealed forever. Ibn Tūmart further based his legitimacy on his claim to be a sharif (descendant of Muhammad) and the *mahdī*, not in the Shīʿite sense but in the more general sense of a human sent to restore pure faith. In his view, Almoravid students of legal knowledge were so concerned with pursuing the technicalities of the law that they had lost the purifying fervour of their own founder, Ibn Yāsīn. They even failed to maintain proper Muslim behaviour, be it the veiling of women in public or the condemning of the use of wine, musical instruments, and other unacceptable, if not strictly illegal, forms of pleasure.

Like many Muslim revitalizers before and since, Ibn Tūmart decried the way in which the law had taken on a life of its own, and he called upon Muslims to rely on the original and only reliable sources, the Qurʾān and Hadith. Although he opposed irresponsible rationalism in the law, in matters of theological discourse he leaned toward the limited rationalism of the Ashʿarite school, which was becoming so popular in the eastern Muslim lands. Like the Ashʿarites, he viewed the unity of God as one of Islam's fundamentals and denounced any reading of the Qurʾān that led to anthropomorphism. Because he focused on attesting the unity of God (*tawḥīd*), he called his followers al-Muwaḥḥidūn (Almohads), "Those Who Attest the Unity of God." Ibn Tūmart's movement signifies the degree to which Maghribis could participate in the intellectual life of Islamdom as a whole, but his need to use the Tamazight language for his many followers who did not know Arabic also illustrates the limits of interregional discourse.

The Almohad Dynasty

By 1147, 17 years after Ibn Tūmart's death, Almohads had replaced Almoravids in all their Maghribi and Andalusian territories. In Andalusia their arrival slowed the progress of the Christian Reconquista. There, as in the Maghrib, arts and letters were encouraged; an example is an important movement of *falsafah* that included Ibn Ṭufayl, Ibn al-ʿArabī, and Ibn Rushd (Latin Averroës), the Andalusian *qāḍī* and physician whose interpretations of Aristotle became so important for medieval European Christianity. During the late Almohad period in Andalusia the intercommunal nature of Islamicate civilization became especially noticeable in the work of non-Muslim thinkers, such as Moses Maimonides, who participated in trends outside their own communities even at the expense of criticism from within. By the early 13th century, Almohad power began to decline; a defeat in 1212 at Las Navas de Tolosa by the Christian kings of the north forced a retreat to the Maghrib. But the impact of Almohad cultural patronage on Andalusia long outlasted Almohad political power; successor dynasties in surviving Muslim states were responsible for some of the highest cultural achievements of Andalusian Muslims, among them the Alhambra palace in Granada. Furthermore, the 400-year southward movement of the Christian-Muslim frontier resulted, ironically, in some of the most intense Christian-Muslim interaction in Andalusian history. The Cid could fight for both sides; Muslims, as Mudejars, could live under Christian rule and contribute to its culture; Jews could translate Arabic and Hebrew texts into Castilian. Almohads were replaced in the Maghrib as well, through a revolt by their own governors—the Ḥafṣids in Tunis and the Marīnid Amazigh dynasty in Fès. There too, however, Almohad influence outlasted their political presence: both towns became centres, in distinctively Maghribi form, of Islamicate culture and Islamic piety.

Continued Spread of Islamic Influence

As the Maghrib became firmly and distinctively Muslim, Islam moved south. The spread of Muslim identity into the Sahara and the involvement of Muslim peoples, especially the Tuareg, in trans-Saharan trade provided several natural channels of influence. By the time of the Marīnids, Ḥafṣids, and Mamlūks, several major trade routes had established crisscrossing lines of communication: from Cairo to Timbuktu, from Tripoli to Bornu and Lake Chad, from Tunis to Timbuktu at the bend of the Niger River, and from Fès and Tafilalt through major Saharan entrepôts into Ghana and Mali. The rise at Timbuktu of Mali, the first great western Sudanic empire with a Muslim ruler, attested the growing incorporation of sub-Saharan Africa into the North African orbit. The reign of Mansa Mūsā, who even went on a pilgrimage, demonstrated the influence of Islam on at least the upper echelons of African society.

The Djinguereber (Djingareyber) Mosque, or Great Mosque, in Timbuktu, Mali, is one of western Africa's oldest mosques.

The best picture of Islamdom in the 14th century appears in the work of a remarkable Maghribi *qāḍī* and traveler, Ibn Baṭṭūṭah (1304–1368/69 or 1377). In 1325, the year that Mansa Mūsā went on his pilgrimage, Ibn Baṭṭūṭah also left for Mecca, from his hometown of Tangiers. He was away for almost 30 years, visiting most of Islamdom, including Andalusia, all of the Maghrib, Mali, Syria, Arabia, Iran, India, the Maldive Islands, and, he claimed, China. He described the unity within diversity that was one of Islamdom's most prominent features. Although local customs often seemed at variance with his notion of pure Islamic practice, he felt at home everywhere. Despite the divisions that had occurred during Islam's 700-year history, a Muslim could attend the Friday worship session in any Muslim town in the world and feel comfortable, a claim that is difficult if not impossible to make for any other major religious tradition at any time in its history.

By the time of Ibn Baṭṭūṭah's death, Islamdom comprised the most far-flung yet interconnected set of societies in the world. As one author has pointed out, Thomas Aquinas (*c.* 1224–74) might have been read from Spain to Hungary and from Sicily to Norway, but Ibn al-ʿArabī (1165–1240) was read from Spain to Sumatra and from the Swahili coast to Kazan on the Volga River. By the end of the period of migration and renewal, Islam had begun to spread not only into sub-Saharan Africa, but also into the southern seas with the establishment of a Muslim presence in the Straits of Malacca. Conversion to Islam across its newer frontiers was at first limited to a small elite who supplemented local religious practices with Muslim ones. Islam could offer not only a unifying religious system, but also social techniques, including alphabetic literacy, a legal system applicable to daily life, a set of administrative institutions, and a body of science and technology—all capable of enhancing the power of ruling elements and of tying them into a vast and lucrative trading network.

The period of migration and renewal exposed both the potentiality and the limitations of government by tribal peoples. This great problem of Islamicate history received its most sophisticated analysis from a Maghribi Muslim named Ibn Khaldūn (1332–1406), a contemporary of Petrarch. His family had migrated from Andalusia to the Maghrib, and he himself was born in Ḥafṣid territory. He was both a *faylasūf* and a *qāḍī*, a combination more common in Andalusia and the Maghrib than anywhere else in Islamdom. His *falsafah* was activist; he strove to use his political wisdom to the benefit of one of the actual rulers of the day. To this end he moved from one court to another before becoming disillusioned and retiring to Mamlūk Cairo as a *qāḍī*. His life thus demonstrated the importance and the constraints of royal patronage as a stimulant to intellectual creativity. In his *Muqaddimah* (the introduction to his multivolume world history) he used his training in *falsafah* to discern patterns in history.

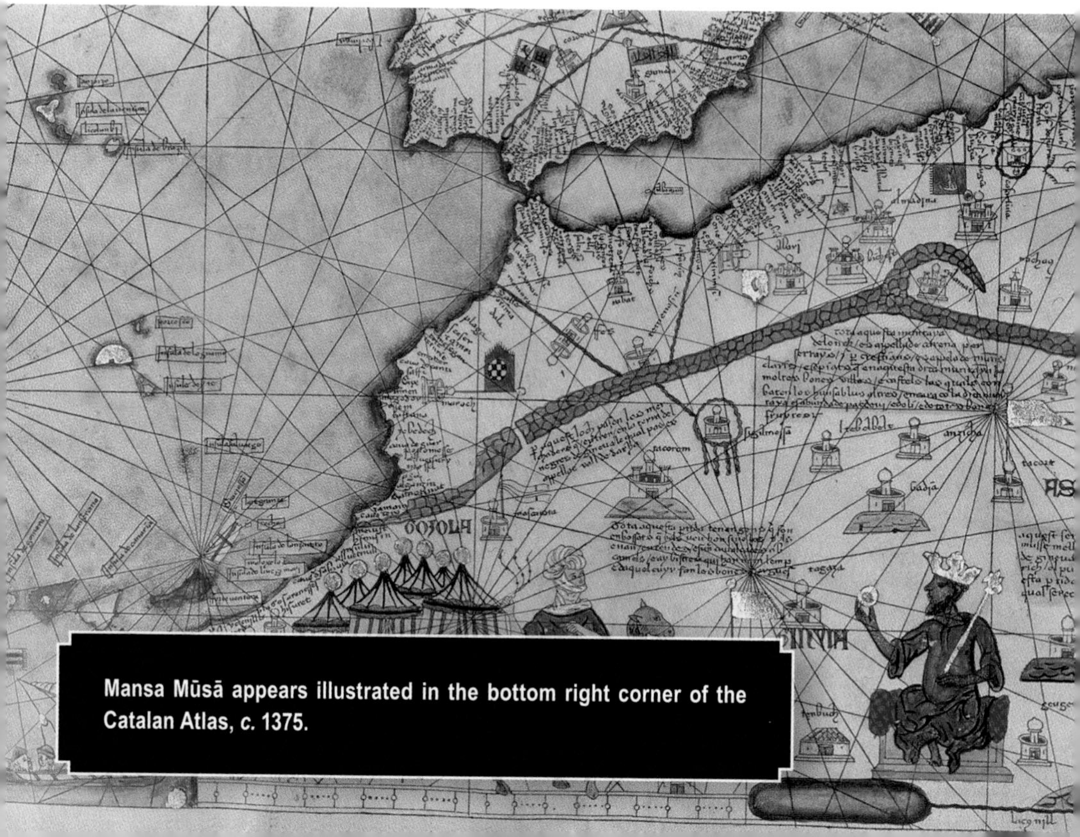

Mansa Mūsā appears illustrated in the bottom right corner of the Catalan Atlas, *c.* 1375.

Transcending the critiques of historical method made by historians of the Būyid period, such as al-Masʿūdī, Ibn Miskawayh, and al-Ṣūlī, Ibn Khaldūn established careful standards of evidence. Whereas Muslim historians conventionally subscribed to the view that God passed sovereignty and hegemony (*dawlah*) from one dynasty to another through his divine wisdom, Ibn Khaldūn explained it in terms of a cycle of natural and inevitable stages. By his day it had become apparent that tribally organized migratory peoples, so favoured by much of the ecology of the Maghrib and the Nile-to-Oxus region, could easily acquire military superiority over settled peoples if they could capitalize on the inherently stronger group feeling (*ʿaṣabiyyah*) that kinship provides. Once in power, according to Ibn Khaldūn, conquering groups pass through a phase in which a small number of "builders" among them bring renewed vitality to their conquered lands. As the family disperses itself among sedentary peoples and ceases to live the hard life of migration, it becomes soft from the prosperity it has brought and begins to degenerate. Then internal rivalries and jealousies force one member of the family to become a king who must rely on mercenary troops and undermine his own prosperity by paying for them. In the end, the ruling dynasty falls prey to a new tribal group with fresh group feeling. Thus did Ibn Khaldūn call attention to the unavoidable instability of all premodern Muslim dynasties, caused by their lack of the regularized patterns of succession that were beginning to develop in European dynasties.

CHAPTER 2

CONSOLIDATION AND EXPANSION (1405–1683)

After the death of Timur in 1405, power began to shift from migrating peoples to sedentary populations living in large centralized empires. After about 1683, when the last Ottoman campaign against Vienna failed, the great empires for which this period is so famous began to shrink and weaken, just as western Europeans first began to show their potential for worldwide expansion and domination. When the period began, Muslim lands had begun to recover from the devastating effects of the plague (1346–48), and many were prospering. Muslims had the best opportunity in history to unite the settled world, but by the end of the period they had been replaced by Europeans as the leading contenders for this role. Muslims were now forced into direct and repeated contact with Europeans, through armed hostilities as well as through commercial interactions, and often the Europeans competed well. Yet Muslim power was so extensive, and the western Europeans such an unexpected source of competition, that Muslims were able to realize that their situation had changed only after they no longer had the strength to resist. Furthermore, the existence of several strong competitive Muslim states militated against a united response to the Europeans and could even encourage some Muslims to align themselves with the European enemies of others.

In this period, long after Islamdom was once thought to have peaked, centralized absolutism reached its height, aided in part by the exploitation of gunpowder warfare and in part by new ways to fuse spiritual and military authority. Never before had Islamicate ideals and institutions better demonstrated their ability to encourage political centralization or to support a Muslim style of life where there was no organized state, be it in areas where Islam had been long established or in areas where it was newly arrived. The major states of this period impressed contemporary Europeans; in them some of the greatest Islamicate artistic achievements were made. In this period Muslims formed the cultural patterns that they brought into modern times, and adherence to Islam expanded to approximately its current distribution. As adherence to Islam expanded, far-flung cultural regions began to take on a life of their own. The unity of several of these regions was expressed through empire—the Ottomans in southeastern Europe, Anatolia, the eastern Maghrib, Egypt, and Syria; the Ṣafavids in Iran and Iraq; the Indo-Timurids (Mughals) in India. In these empires, Sunni and Shīʿite became identities on a much larger scale than ever before, expressing competition between large populations; simultaneously Shīʿism acquired a permanent base from which to generate international opposition.

Elsewhere, less formal and often commercial ties bound Muslims from distant locales; growing commercial and political links between Morocco and the western Sudan produced a trans-Saharan Maghribi Islam; Egyptian Islam influenced the central and eastern Sudan; and steady contacts between East Africa, South Arabia, southern Iran, southwest India, and the southern seas promoted a recognizable Indian Ocean Islam, with Persian as its lingua franca. In fact, Persian became the closest yet to an international language; but the expansion and naturalization of Islam also fostered a number of local languages into vehicles for Islamicate administration and high culture—Ottoman, Chagatai, Swahili, Urdu, and Malay. Everywhere Muslims were confronting adherents of other religions, and new converts often practiced Islam without abandoning their previous practices. The various ways in which Muslims responded to religious syncretism and plurality continue to be elaborated to the present day.

This was a period of major realignments and expansion. The extent of Muslim presence in the Eastern Hemisphere in the early 15th century was easily discernible, but only with difficulty could one have imagined that it could soon produce three of the greatest empires in world history. From the Atlantic to the Pacific, from the Balkans to Sumatra, Muslim rulers presided over relatively small kingdoms, but nowhere could the emergence of a world-class dynasty be predicted. In Andalusia only one Muslim state, Granada, remained to resist Christian domination of the Iberian Peninsula. The Maghrib, isolated between an almost all-Christian Iberia and an eastward-looking Mamlūk Egypt and Syria, was divided between the Marīnids and Ḥafṣids. Where the Sahara shades off into the Sudanic belt, the empire of Mali at Gao was ruled by a Muslim and included several Saharan "port" cities, such as Timbuktu, that were centres of Muslim learning. On the Swahili coast, oriented as always more toward the Indian Ocean than toward its own hinterland, several small Muslim polities centred on key ports such as Kilwa.

In western Anatolia and the Balkan Peninsula the Ottoman state under Sultan Mehmed I was recovering from its defeat by Timur. Iraq and western Iran were the domains of Turkic tribal dynasties known as the Black Sheep (Kara Koyunlu) and the White Sheep (Ak Koyunlu); they shared a border in Iran with myriad princelings of the Timurid line, and the neo-Mongol, neo-Timurid Uzbek state ruled in Transoxania. North of the Caspian, several Muslim khanates ruled as far north as Moscow and Kazan. In India, even though Muslims constituted a minority, they were beginning to assert their power everywhere except the south, which was ruled by Vijayanagar. In Islamdom's far southeast, the Muslim state of Samudra held sway in Sumatra, and the rulers of the Moluccas had recently converted to Islam and begun to expand into the southern Malay Peninsula.

Even where no organized state existed, as in the outer reaches of Central Asia and into southern China, scattered small Muslim communities persisted, often centred on oases. By the end of this period, Islamdom's borders had retreated only in Russia and Iberia, but these losses were more than compensated for by continuing expansion in Europe, Africa, Central Asia, and South and Southeast Asia. Almost everywhere this plethora of states had undergone realignment and consolidation, based on experimentation with forms of legitimation and structure.

OTTOMANS

After the Ottoman state's devastating defeat by Timur, its leaders had to retain the vitality of the warrior spirit (without its unruliness and intolerance) and the validation of the Sharīʿah (without its confining independence). In 1453 Mehmed II (the Conqueror) fulfilled the warrior ideal by conquering Constantinople (soon to be known as Istanbul), putting an end to the Byzantine Empire, and subjugating the local Christian and Jewish

Mehmed II, miniature from the 17th-century *Turkish Memories*, Arabic manuscript, *Cicogna Codex*; in Museo Correr, Venice, Italy.

populations. Even by then, however, a new form of legitimation was taking shape.

Continuation of Ottoman Rule

The Ottomans continued to wage war against Christians on the frontier and to levy and convert young male Christians to serve in the sultan's household and army (through the *devşirme*, Christian youths converted to Islam and put through special training at the capital to be the sultan's personal "slaves"). However, warriors were being pensioned off with land grants and replaced by troops more beholden to the sultan. Except for those forcibly converted, the rest of the non-Muslim population was protected for payment according to the Sharīʿah and the preference of the *ulema* (the Turkish spelling of *ulama*), and organized into self-governing communities known as *millets*. Furthermore, the sultans began to claim the caliphate because they met two of its traditional qualifications: they ruled justly, in principle according to the Sharīʿah, and they defended and extended the frontiers, as in their conquest of Mamlūk Egypt, Syria, and the holy cities in 1516–17.

Meanwhile, they began to undercut the traditional oppositional stance of the *ulema* by building on Seljuq and Mongol practice in three ways: they promoted state-supported training of *ulema*; they defined and paid holders of religious offices as part of the military; and they aggressively asserted the validity of dynastic law alongside Sharīʿah. Simultaneously, they emphasized their inheritance of Byzantine legitimacy by transforming Byzantine symbols, such as Hagia Sophia (Church of the Divine Wisdom), into symbols for Islam, and by favouring their empire's European part, called, significantly, Rūm.

Hagia Sophia (Church of the Divine Wisdom) is one example of an icon of Byzantine culture transformed into a symbol of Islam by the Ottomans.

REIGN OF SÜLEYMAN I

The classical Ottoman system crystallized during the reign of Süleyman I (the Lawgiver; ruled 1520–66). He also pushed the empire's borders almost to their farthest limits—to the walls of Vienna in the northwest, throughout the Maghrib up to Morocco in the southwest, into Iraq to the east, and to the Yemen in the southeast. During Süleyman's reign the Ottomans even sent an expedition into the southern seas to help Aceh against the Portuguese colonizers.

In theory, Süleyman presided over a balanced four-part structure: the palace household, which contained all of the sultan's wives, concubines, children, and servants; the bureaucracy (chancery and treasury); the armed forces; and the religious establishment. Important positions in the army and bureaucracy went to the cream of the *devşirme*. *Ulema* who acquired government posts had undergone systematic training at the major *medreses* (*madrasas*) and so in the Ottoman state were more integrated than were their counterparts in other states; yet they were freeborn Muslims, not brought into the system as slaves of the sultan. The ruling class communicated in a language developed for their use only, Ottoman, which combined Turkic syntax with largely Arabic and Persian vocabulary. It was in this new language that so many important figures demonstrated the range and sophistication of Ottoman interests, such as the historian Mustafa Naima, the encyclopaedist Kâtip Çelebi, and the traveler Evliya Çelebi. The splendour of the Ottoman capital owed not a little to Süleyman's chief architect, the Greek *devşirme* recruit Sinan, who transformed the city's skyline with magnificent mosques and *medreses*.

THE EXTENT OF OTTOMAN ADMINISTRATION

Even in North Africa and the Fertile Crescent, where Ottoman rule was indirect, the effect of its administration, especially its land surveys and *millet* and tax systems, could be felt; remnants of the Ottoman system continue to play a role in the political life of modern states such as Israel and Lebanon, despite the fact that Ottoman control had already begun to relax by the first quarter of the 17th century. By then control of the state treasury was passing, through land grants, into the hands of local *aʿyān*, and they gradually became the real rulers, serving

At its greatest extent, the Ottoman Empire controlled lands in Europe, Africa, and Asia.

local rather than imperial interests. Meanwhile, discontinuance of the *devşirme* and the rise of hereditary succession to imperial offices shut off new sources of vitality. Monarchs, confined to the palace during their youth, became weaker and participated less in military affairs and government councils.

As early as 1630, Sultan Murad IV was presented by one of his advisers with a memorandum explaining the causes of the perceived decline and urging a restoration of the system as it had existed under Süleyman. Murad IV tried to restore Ottoman efficiency and central control, and his efforts were continued by subsequent sultans aided by a talented family of ministers known as the Köprülüs. However, during a war with the Holy League (Austria, Russia, Venice, and Poland) from 1683 to 1699, in which a major attack on Vienna failed (1683), the Ottomans suffered their first serious losses to an enemy and exposed the weakness of their system to their European neighbours. They signed two treaties, at Carlowitz in 1699 and at Passarowitz in 1718, that confirmed their losses in southeastern Europe, signified their inferiority to the Habsburg coalition, and established the defensive posture they would maintain into the 20th century.

Ṣafavids

The Ṣafavid state began not from a band of *ghāzī* warriors but from a local Sufi *ṭarīqah* of Ardabīl in the Azerbaijan region of Iran. The *ṭarīqah* was named after its founder, Shaykh Ṣafī al-Dīn (1252/53–1334), a local holy man. As for many *ṭarīqahs* and other voluntary associations, Sunni and Shīʿite alike, affection for the family of ʿAlī was a channel for popular support. During the 15th century Shaykh Ṣafī's successors transformed their local *ṭarīqah* into an interregional movement by translating ʿAlid loyalism into full-fledged Imāmī Shīʿism. By asserting that they were the Sufi "perfect men" of their time, as well as descendants and representatives of the last imam, they strengthened the support of their Turkic tribal disciples (known as the Kizilbash, or "Red Heads," because of their symbolic 12-fold red headgear). They also attracted support outside Iran, especially in eastern Anatolia (where the anti-Ottoman Imāmī Bekṭāshī *ṭarīqah* was strong), in Syria, the Caucasus, and Transoxania. The ability of the Iranian Shīʿite state to serve as a source of widespread local opposition outside of Iran was again to become dramatically apparent many years later, with the rise of the Ayatollah Ruhollah Khomeini's Islamic republic in the late 1970s.

EXPANSION IN IRAN AND BEYOND

By 1501 the Ṣafavids were able to defeat the Ak Koyunlu rulers of northern Iran, whereupon their teenage leader Ismāʿīl I (ruled 1501–24) had himself proclaimed shah, using that pre-Islamic title for the first time in almost 900 years and thereby invoking the glory of ancient Iran. The Ṣafavids thus asserted a multipronged legitimacy that flew in the face of Ottoman claims to have restored caliphal authority for all Muslims. Eventually, irritant became threat: by 1510, when Ismāʿīl had conquered all of Iran (to approximately its present frontiers) as well as the Fertile Crescent, he began pushing against the Uzbeks in the east and the Ottomans in the west, both of whom already suffered from significant Shīʿite opposition that could easily be aroused by Ṣafavid successes. Having to fight on two fronts was the most difficult military problem any Muslim empire could face. According to the persisting Mongol pattern, the army was a single force attached to the household of the ruler and moving with him at all times; so the size of an area under effective central control was limited to the farthest points that could be reached in a single campaign season.

After dealing with his eastern front, Ismāʿīl turned west. At Chāldirān (1514) in northwestern Iraq, having refused to use gunpowder weapons, Ismāʿīl suffered the kind of defeat at Ottoman hands that the Ottomans had suffered from Timur. Yet through the war of words waged in a body of correspondence between Shah Ismāʿīl and the Ottoman sultan Selim I, and through the many invasions from both fronts that occurred during the next 60 years, the Ṣafavid state survived and prospered. Still living off its position at the crossroads of the trans-Asian trade that had supported all previous empires in Iraq and Iran, it was not yet undermined by the gradual emergence of more significant sea routes to the south.

The first requirement for the survival of the Ṣafavid state was the conversion of its predominantly Jamāʿī-Sunni population to Imāmī Shīʿism. This was accomplished by a government-run effort supervised by the state-appointed leader of the religious community, the *ṣadr*. Gradually forms of piety emerged that were specific to Ṣafavid Shīʿism; they centred on pilgrimage to key sites connected with the imams, as well as on the annual remembering and reenacting of the key event in Shīʿite history, the caliph Yazīd I's destruction of Imam al-Ḥusayn at Karbalāʾ on the 10th of Muḥarram, AH 61 (680 CE). The 10th of Muḥarram, or ʿĀshūrāʾ, already marked throughout Islamdom with fasting, became for Iranian Shīʿites the centre of the religious calendar. The first 10 days of Muḥarram became a period of communal mourning during which the pious imposed suffering on themselves to identify with their martyrs of old, listened to sermons, and recited appropriate elegiac poetry. In later Ṣafavid times the name for this mourning, *taʿziyyeh*, also came to be applied to passion plays performed to reenact events surrounding al-Ḥusayn's martyrdom. Through the depths of their empathetic suffering, Shīʿites could help to overturn the injustice of al-Ḥusayn's martyrdom at the end of time, when all wrongs would be righted, all wrongdoers punished, and all true followers of the imams rewarded.

Shah ʿAbbās I

The state also survived because Ismāʿīl's successors moved, like the Ottomans, toward a type of legitimation different from the one that had brought them to power. This development began in the reign of Ṭahmāsp (1524–76) and culminated in the reign of the greatest Ṣafavid shah, ʿAbbās I (ruled 1588–1629). Since Ismāʿīl's time, the tribes had begun to lose faith in the Ṣafavid monarch as spiritual leader;

'Abbās I, detail of a painting by the Mughal school of Jahangir, *c.* 1620; in the Freer Gallery of Art, Washington, D.C.

now ʿAbbās appealed for support more as absolute monarch and less as the charismatic Sufi master or incarnated imam. At the same time, he freed himself from his unruly tribal emirs by depending more and more on a paid army of converted Circassian, Georgian, and Armenian Christian captives.

Meanwhile, he continued to rely on a large bureaucracy headed by a chief minister with limited responsibilities, but, unlike his Ottoman contemporaries, he distanced members of the religious community from state involvement while allowing them an independent source of support in their administration of the *waqf* (land held in trust and dedicated to charitable or educational purposes) system. Because the Shīʿite ulama had a tradition of independence that made them resist incorporation into the military "household" of the shah, ʿAbbās's policies were probably not unpopular, but they eventually undermined his state's legitimacy. By the end of the period under discussion, it was the religious leaders, the *mujtahids*, who would claim to be the spokesmen for the hidden imam. Having shared the ideals of the military patronage state, the Ottoman state became more firmly militarized and religious, as the Ṣafavid became more civilianized and secular. The long-term consequences of this breach between government and the religious institution were extensive, culminating in the establishment of the Islamic republic of Iran in 1978.

ʿAbbās expressed his new role by moving his capital about 1597–98 to Eṣfahān in Fārs, the central province of the ancient pre-Islamic Iranian empires and symbolically more Persian than Turkic. Eṣfahān, favoured by a high and scenic setting, became one of the most beautiful cities in the world, leading its boosters to say that "Eṣfahān is half the world." It came to contain, often thanks to royal patronage, myriad palaces, gardens, parks, mosques, *medreses*, caravansaries, workshops, and public baths. Many of these still stand, including the famed Masjed-e Shah, a mosque that shares the great central mall with an enormous covered bazaar and many other structures. It was there that

The Masjed-e Shah (Shah's Mosque) in Eṣfahān, constructed following ʿAbbās's establishment of Eṣfahān as the Ṣafavid capital in 1597–98, still stands today.

ʿAbbās received diplomatic and commercial visits from Europeans, including a Carmelite mission from Pope Clement XIII (1604) and the adventuring Sherley brothers from Elizabethan England. Just as his visitors hoped to use him to their own advantage, ʿAbbās hoped to use them to his—as sources of firearms and military technology, or as pawns in his economic warfare against the Ottomans, in which he was willing to seek help from apparently anyone, including the Russians, Portuguese, and Habsburgs.

Under Ṣafavid rule, Iran in the 16th and 17th centuries became the centre of a major cultural flowering expressed through the Persian language and through the visual arts. This flowering extended to Ṣafavid neighbour states as well—Ottomans, Uzbeks, and Indo-Timurids. Like other Shīʿite dynasties before them, the Ṣafavids encouraged the development of *falsafah* as a companion to Shīʿite esotericism and cosmology. Two major thinkers, Mīr Dāmād and his disciple Mullā Ṣadrā, members of the Ishrāqī, or illuminationist, school, explored the realm of images or symbolic imagination as a way to understand issues of human meaningfulness. The Ṣafavid period was also important for the development of Shīʿite Sharīʿah-minded studies, and it produced a major historian, Iskandar Beg Munshī, chronicler of ʿAbbās's reign.

Decline of Central Authority

None of ʿAbbās's successors was his equal, though his state, ever weaker, survived for a century. The last effective shah, Ḥusayn I (1694–1722), could defend himself neither from tribal raiding in the capital nor from interfering *mujtahids* led by Muḥammad Bāqir Majlisī (whose writings later would be important in the Islamic republic of Iran). In 1722, when Maḥmūd of Qandahār led an Afghan tribal raid into Iran from the east, he easily took Eṣfahān and destroyed what was left of central authority.

Indo-Timurids (Mughals)

Although the Mongol-Timurid legacy influenced the Ottoman and Ṣafavid states, it had its most direct impact on Bābur (1483–1530), the famed adventurer and founder of the third major empire of the period.

Foundation by Bābur

Bābur's father, ʿUmar Shaykh Mīrzā (died 1494) of Fergana, was one among many Timurid "princes" who continued to rule small pieces of the lands their great ancestor had conquered. After his father's death, the 11-year-old Bābur, who claimed descent not only from Timur but also from Genghis Khan (on his mother's side), quickly faced one of the harshest realities of his time and place—too many princes for too few kingdoms. In his youth he dreamed of capturing Samarkand as a base for reconstructing Timur's empire. For a year after the Ṣafavid defeat of the Uzbek Muḥammad Shaybānī Khān, Bābur and his Chagatai followers did hold Samarkand, as Ṣafavid vassals, but, when the Ṣafavids were in turn defeated, Bābur lost not only Samarkand but his native Fergana as well. He was forced to retreat to Kabul, which he had occupied in 1504. From there he never restored Timur's empire; rather, barred from moving north or west, he took the Timurid legacy south, to a land on which Timur had made only the slightest impression.

When Bābur turned toward northern India, it was ruled from Delhi by the Lodī sultans, one of many local Turkic dynasties scattered through the subcontinent. In 1526 at Pānīpat, Bābur met and defeated the much larger Lodī army. In his victory he was aided, like the Ottomans at Chāldirān, by his artillery. By his death just four years later, he had laid the foundation for a remarkable empire, known most commonly as the Mughal (i.e., Mongol) Empire. It is more properly called Indo-Timurid because the Chagatai Turks were distinct from the surviving Mongols of the time and because Bābur and his successors acknowledge Timur as the founder of their power.

Bābur is also remembered for his memoirs, the *Bābur-n āmeh.* Written in Chagatai, then an emerging Islamicate literary language, his work gives a lively and compelling account of the wide range of interests, tastes, and sensibilities that made him so much a counterpart of his contemporary, the Italian Niccolò Machiavelli (1469–1527).

Akbar, miniature portrait from the *Akbar-nameh* by Abu al-Faḍl, *c.* 1600; in the India Office Library, London.

Reign of Akbar

Süleyman's and ʿAbbās's counterpart in the Indo-Timurid dynasty was their contemporary, Akbar (ruled 1556–1605), the grandson of Bābur. At the time of his death, he ruled all of present-day India north of the Deccan plateau and Gondwana and more: one diagonal of his empire extended from the Hindu Kush to the Bay of Bengal; the other, from the Himalayas to the Arabian Sea. Like its contemporaries to the west, particularly the Ottomans, this state endured because of a regularized and equitable tax system that provided the central treasury with funds to support the ruler's extensive building projects as well as his *manṣabdārs*, the military and bureaucratic officers of the imperial service. For these key servants, Akbar, again like his counterparts to the west, relied largely on foreigners who were trained especially for his service. Like the Janissaries, the *manṣabdārs* were not supposed to inherit their offices, and, although they were assigned lands to supervise, they themselves were paid through the central treasury to assure their loyalty to the interests of the ruler.

MANṢABDĀRS

The *manṣabdārs* were members of the imperial bureaucracy of the Mughal Empire in India who governed the empire and commanded its armies in the emperor's name. Though they were usually aristocrats, they did not form a feudal aristocracy, for neither the offices nor the estates that supported them were hereditary. The system was organized by the emperor Akbar (reigned 1556–1605), who shaped a loose military confederation of Muslim nobles into a multiethnic bureaucratic empire integrating Muslims and Hindus. The word is of Arabic origin, *dār* indicating the holder of an office or dignity and *manṣab* being a rank determined by the command of a specified number of men. There were 33 grades ranging from 10 to 5,000 (the highest for a subject) in a complicated system. For the maintenance of the men, the *manṣabdārs* received a salary, which Akbar paid in cash but which later emperors met by means of assignments on the revenues. The lands thus assigned were liable to transfer during a *manṣabdār's* lifetime and were taken back at his death. To pay his way the *manṣabdār* was allowed advances from the treasury, which at death were recoverable in what amounted to a death duty of 100 percent.

Manṣabdārs held military commands and civil posts. The system provided an outlet for ambition and ability within the imperial service and formed the framework of the Mughal administration. The *manṣabdārs* were controlled by their dependence on salaries, by frequent transfer from one appointment to another, and by the diversion of revenue collection direct to the treasury. They had therefore little opportunity to build up either local connections or financial resources for raising private armies. For much of the Mughal period, the *manṣabdārs* were mostly of foreign origin or extraction, as were 70 percent of them toward the end of Akbar's reign. The remaining 30 percent were divided about equally between Muslims and Hindus, of which the latter were mainly Rajputs.

Although Akbar's empire was, like Süleyman's and ʿAbbās's, a variation on the theme of the military patronage state, his situation, and consequently many of his problems, differed from theirs in important ways. Islam was much more recently established in most of his empire than in either of the other two, and Muslims were not in the majority. Although the other two states were not religiously or ethnically homogeneous, the extent of their internal diversity could not compare with Akbar's, where Muslims and non-Muslims of every stripe alternately coexisted and came into conflict—Jacobites (members of the monophysite Syrian church), Sufis, Ismāʿīlī Shīʿites, Zoroastrians, Jains, Jesuits, Jews, and Hindus. Consequently, Akbar was forced even more than the Ottomans to confront and address the issue of religious plurality. The option of aggressive conversion was virtually impossible in such a vast area, as was any version of the Ottoman *millet* system in a setting in which hundreds if not thousands of *millets* could be defined.

In some ways, Akbar faced in exaggerated form the situation that the Arab Muslims faced when they were a minority in the Nile-to-Oxus region in the 7th–9th centuries. Granting protected status to non-Muslims, even those who were not really "Peoples of the Book" in the original sense, with an organized religion of their own, was legally and administratively justifiable, but unless they could be kept from interacting too much with the Muslim population, Islam itself could be affected. The power of Sufi *ṭarīqahs* like the influential Chishtīs, and of the Hindu mystical movement of Guru Nānak, were already promoting intercommunal interaction and cross-fertilization. Akbar's response was different from that of the ʿAbbāsid caliph al-Maḥdi. Instead of institutionalizing intolerance of non-Muslim influences and instead of hardening communal lines, Akbar banned intolerance and even the special tax on non-Muslims. To keep the ulama from objecting, he tried, for different reasons than had the Ottomans and

Ṣafavids, to tie them to the state financially. His personal curiosity about other religions was exemplary; with the help of Abu al-Faḍl, his Sufi adviser and biographer, he established a kind of salon for religious discussion. A very small circle of personal disciples seems to have emulated Akbar's own brand of *tawḥīd-i ilāhī* ("divine oneness"). This appears to have been a general monotheism akin to what the *ḥanīfs* of Mecca and Muhammad himself had once practiced, as well as to the boundary-breaking pantheistic awareness of great Sufis like Rūmī and Ibn al-ʿArabī, who was very popular in South and Southeast Asia. Akbar combined toleration for all religions with condemnation of practices that seemed to him humanly objectionable, such as enslavement and the immolation of widows.

Continuation of the Empire

For half a century, Akbar's first two successors, Jahāngīr and Shah Jahān, continued his policies. A rebuilt capital at Delhi was added to the old capitals of Fatehpur Sikri and Agra, site of Shah Jahān's most famous building, the Taj Mahal. The mingling of Hindu and Muslim traditions was expressed in all the arts, especially in naturalistic and sensuous painting; extremely refined and sophisticated design in ceramics, inlay work, and textiles; and in delicate yet monumental architecture. Shah Jahān's son, Dārā Shikōh (1615–59), was a Sufi thinker and writer who tried to establish a common ground for Muslims and Hindus. In response to such attempts, a Sharīʿah-minded movement of strict communalism arose, connected with a leader of the Naqshbandī *ṭarīqah* named Shaykh Aḥmad Sirhindī. With the accession of Aurangzeb (ruled 1658–1707), the tradition of ardent ecumenicism, which would reemerge several centuries later in a non-Muslim named Mohandas K. (Mahatma) Gandhi, was replaced with a stricter

Aladdin Saluted Her with Joy, illustration by Virginia Frances Sterrett from *Arabian Nights* (1928).

communalism that imposed penalties on protected non-Muslims and stressed the shah's role as leader of the Muslim community, by virtue of his enforcing the Sharīʿah. Unlike the Ottoman and Ṣafavid domains, the Indo-Timurid empire was still expanding right up to the beginning of the 18th century, but the empire began to disintegrate shortly after the end of Aurangzeb's reign, when Ṣafavid and Ottoman power were also declining rapidly.

Between the 15th and the 18th century the use of coffee, tea, and tobacco, despite the objections of the ulama, became common in all three empires. Teahouses became important new centres for male socializing, in addition to the home, the mosque, the marketplace, and the public bath. (Female socializing was restricted largely to the home and the bath.) In the teahouses men could practice the already well-developed art of storytelling and take delight in the clever use of language. *The Thousand and One Nights* (*Alf laylah wa laylah*), the earliest extant manuscripts of which date from this period, and the stories of the Arabian hero ʿAntar must have been popular, as were the tales of a wise fool known as Mullah Naṣr al-Dīn in Persian (Nasreddin), Hoca in Turkish, and Juḥā in Arabic. The exploits of Naṣr al-Dīn, sometimes in the guise of a Sufi dervish or royal adviser, often humorously portray centralized absolutism and mysticism:

> Naṣr al-Dīn was sent by the King to investigate the lore of various kinds of Eastern mystical teachers. They all recounted to him tales of the miracles and the sayings of the founders and great teachers, all long dead, of their schools. When he returned home, he submitted his report, which contained the single word "Carrots." He was called upon to explain himself. Naṣr al-Dīn told the King: "The best part is buried; few know—except the farmer—by the green that there is orange underground; if you don't work for it, it will deteriorate; there are a great many donkeys associated with it."

Trans-Saharan Islam

When the Ottomans expanded through the southern Mediterranean coast in the early 16th century, they were unable to incorporate Morocco, where a new state had been formed in reaction to the appearance of the Portuguese. The Portuguese were riding the momentum generated by their own seaborne expansion as well as by the fulfillment of the Reconquista and the establishment of an aggressively intolerant Christian regime in the centre of the Iberian Peninsula. In Morocco it was neither the fervour of warriors nor Shīʿite solidarity nor Timurid restoration that motivated the formation of a state; rather, it was a very old form of legitimacy that had proved to be especially powerful in Africa—that of the sharifs, descendants of Muhammad. It had last been relied on with the Idrīsids; now the sharifs were often associated with Sufi holy men, known as marabouts. It was one such Sufi, Sīdī Barakāt, who legitimated the Saʿdī family of sharifs as leaders of a jihad that expelled the Portuguese and established an independent state (1511–1603) strong enough to expand far to the south.

Meanwhile, the greatest Muslim kingdom of the Sudan, Songhai, was expanding northward, and its growing control of major trade routes into Morocco provoked Moroccan interference. Invaded in 1591, Songhai was ruled as a Moroccan vassal for 40 years, during which time Morocco itself was experiencing political confusion and instability. Morocco was reunited under Ismāʿīl (ruled 1672–1727), an ʿAlawite sharif. A holy family of Sijilmassa, the ʿAlawites were brought to power by Arab tribal support, which they eventually had to replace with a costly army of black slaves. Like the Saʿdīs, they were legitimated in two ways: by the recognition of leading Sufis and by the special spiritual quality (*barakah*) presumed to have passed to them by virtue of their descent from the Prophet through ʿAlī. Although they were not Shīʿites, they cultivated charismatic leadership that undermined the power of the ulama to use the Sharīʿah against them. They also recognized the limits of their authority as absolute monarchs, dividing their realm into the area of authority and the area of no authority (where many of the Amazigh tribes lived). Thus, the Moroccan sharifs solved the universal problems of legitimacy, loyalty, and control in a way tailored to their own situation.

While the Saʿdī dynasty was ruling in Morocco but long before its incursions into the Sahara, a number of small Islamic states were strung from one end of the Sudanic region to the other: Senegambia, Songhai, Aïr, Mossi, Nupe, Hausa, Kanem-Bornu, Darfur, and Funj. Islam had come to these areas along trade and pilgrimage routes, especially through the efforts of a number of learned teaching-trading families such as the Kunta. Ordinarily the ruling elites became Muslim first, employing the skills of Arab immigrants, traders, or travelers, and taking political and commercial advantage of the Arabic language and the Sharīʿah without displacing indigenous religious practices or legitimating principles. By the 16th century the Muslim states of the Sudanic belt were in contact not only with the major Muslim centres of the Maghrib and Egypt but also with each other through an emerging trans-Sudanic pilgrimage route. Furthermore, Islam had by then become well enough established to provoke efforts at purification comparable to the Almoravid movement of the 11th century. Sometimes these efforts were gradualist and primarily educational, as was the case with the enormously influential Egyptian scholar al-Suyūṭī (1445–1505). His works, read by many West African Muslims for centuries after his death, dealt with numerous subjects, including the coming of the *mahdī* to restore justice and strengthen Islam. He also wrote letters to Muslim scholars and rulers in West Africa more than 2,000 miles (3,200 km) away, explaining the Sharīʿah and encouraging its careful observance.

Other efforts to improve the observance of Islam were more militant. Rulers might forcibly insist on an end to certain non-Muslim practices, as did Muḥammad Rumfa (ruled 1463–99) in the Hausa city-state of Kano, or Muḥammad I Askia, the greatest ruler of Songhai (ruled 1493–1528). Often, as in the case of both of these rulers, militance was encouraged by an aggressive reformist scholar like al-Maghīlī (flourished 1492), whose writings detailed the conditions that would justify a jihad against Muslims who practiced their faith inadequately. Like many reformers, al-Maghīlī identified himself as a *mujaddid*, a figure expected to appear around the turn of each Muslim century. (The 10th century AH began in 1494 CE.)

To the east in Ethiopia, an actual jihad was carried out by Aḥmad Grāñ (c. 1506–43), in the name of opposition to the Christian regime and purification of "compromised" Islam. Farther to the east, a conquest of Christian Nubia by Arab tribes of Upper Egypt resulted in the conversion of the pagan Funj to Islam and the creation of a major Muslim kingdom there. Although most indigenous West

African scholars looked to foreigners for inspiration, a few began to chart their own course. In Timbuktu, where a rich array of Muslim learning was available, one local scholar and member of a Tukulor learned family, Aḥmad Bābā, was writing works that were of interest to North African Muslims. Local histories written in Arabic also survive, such as the *Taʾrīkh al-fattāsh* (written by several generations of the Kāti family, from 1519 to 1665), a chronological history of Songhai, or al-Saʿdī's *Taʾrīkh al-Sūdān* (completed in 1655). By the end of the period of consolidation and expansion, Muslims in the Sudanic belt were being steadily influenced by North African Islam but were also developing distinctive traditions of their own.

The tomb of Muḥammad I Askia stands in Gao, Mali. As emperor of Songhai (1493–1528), Muḥammad used military power to enforce the observance of Islam.

Indian Ocean Islam

A similar relationship was simultaneously developing across another "sea," the Indian Ocean, which tied South and Southeast Asian Muslims to East African and south Arabian Muslims the way the Sahara linked North African and Sudanic Muslims. Several similarities are clear: the alternation of advance and retreat, the movement of outside influences along trade routes, and the emergence of significant local scholarship. There were differences too: Indian Ocean Muslims had to cope with the Portuguese threat and to face Hindus and Buddhists more than pagans, so that Islam had to struggle against sophisticated and refined religious traditions that possessed written literature and considerable political power.

The first major Muslim state in Southeast Asia, Aceh, was established around 1524 in northern and western Sumatra in response to more than a decade of Portuguese advance. Under Sultan Iskandar Muda (ruled 1607–37), Aceh reached the height of its prosperity and importance in the Indian Ocean trade, encouraging Muslim learning and expanding Muslim adherence. By the end of the 17th century, Aceh's Muslims were in touch with major intellectual centres to the west, particularly in India and Arabia, just as West African Muslims were tied to centres across the Sahara. Because they could draw on many sources, often filtered through India, Sumatran Muslims may have been exposed to a wider corpus of Muslim learning than Muslims in many parts of the heartland. Aceh's scholarly disputes over Ibn al-ʿArabī were even significant enough to attract the attention of a leading Medinan, Ibrāhīm al-Kūrānī, who in 1640 wrote a response. The same kind of naturalization and indigenization of Islam that was taking place in Africa was also taking place here; for example, ʿAbd al-Raʾūf of Singkel, after studying in Arabia from about 1640 to 1661, returned home, where he made the first "translation" of the Qurʾān into

Malay, a language that was much enriched during this period by Arabic script and vocabulary. This phenomenon extended even to China. Liu Xhi, a scholar born around 1650 in Nanking (Nanjing), created serious Islamicate literature in Chinese, including works of philosophy and law.

In the early 17th century another Muslim commercial power emerged when its ruler, the prince of Tallo, converted; Macassar (now Makassar) became an active centre for Muslim competition with the Dutch into the third quarter of the 17th century, when its greatest monarch, Ḥasan al-Dīn (ruled 1631–70), was forced to cede his independence. Meanwhile, however, a serious Islamic presence was developing in Java, inland as well as on the coasts; by the early 17th century the first inland Muslim state in Southeast Asia, Mataram, was established. There Sufi holy men performed a missionary function similar to that being performed in Africa. Unlike the more seriously Islamized states in Sumatra, Mataram suffered, as did its counterparts in West Africa, from its inability to suppress indigenous beliefs to the satisfaction of the more conservative ulama. Javanese Muslims, unlike those in Sumatra, would have to struggle for centuries to negotiate the confrontation between Hindu and Muslim cultures. Their situation underscores a major theme of Islamicate history through the period of consolidation and expansion—that is, the repeatedly demonstrated absorptive capacity of Muslim societies, a capacity that was soon to be challenged in unprecedented ways.

Chapter 3

Precolonial Reform and Dependency (1683 to the Early 20th Century)

The history of modern Islam has often been explained in terms of the impact of "the West." From this perspective the 18th century was a period of degeneration and a prelude to European domination, symbolized by Napoleon I's conquest of Egypt in 1798. Yet it is also possible to argue that the period of Western domination was merely an interlude in the ongoing development of indigenous styles of modernization. In order to resolve this question, it is necessary to begin the "modern" period with the 18th century, when activism and revival were present throughout Islamdom. The three major Muslim empires did experience a decline during the 18th century, as compared with their own earlier power and with the rising powers in Europe, but most Muslims were not yet aware that Europe was partly to blame. Similar decline had occurred many times before, a product of the inevitable weaknesses of the military-conquest state turned into centralized absolutism, overdependence on continuous expansion, weakening of training for rule, the difficulty of maintaining efficiency and loyalty in a large and complex royal household and army, and the difficulty of maintaining sufficient revenues for an increasingly lavish court life. Furthermore, population increased, as it did almost everywhere in the 18th-century world, just as inflation and expensive reform reduced income to central governments. Given the insights of Ibn Khaldūn, however, one might have expected a new group with a fresh sense of cohesiveness to restore political strength.

Had Muslims remained on a par with all other societies, they might have revived. But by the 18th century one particular set of societies in western Europe had developed an economic and social system capable of transcending the 5,000-year-old limitations of the agrarian-based settled world as defined by the Greeks—who called it Oikoumene. Unlike most of the lands of Islamdom, those societies were rich in natural resources (especially the fossil fuels that could supplement human and animal power) and poor in space for expansion. Cut off by Muslims from controlling land routes from the East, European explorers had built on and surpassed Muslim seafaring technology to compete in the southern seas and discover new sea routes—and, accidentally, a new source of wealth in the Americas. In Europe centralized absolutism, though an ideal, had not been the success it was in Islamdom. Emerging from the landed classes rather than from the cities, it had benefited from and been constrained by independent urban commercial classes. In Islamdom the power of merchants had been inhibited by imperial overtaxation of local private enterprise, appropriation of the benefits of trade, and the privileging of foreign traders through agreements known as the Capitulations.

In Europe independent financial and social resources promoted an unusual freedom for technological experimentation and, consequently, the technicalization of other areas of society as well. Unlike previous innovations in the Oikoumene, Europe's technology could not easily be diffused to societies that had not undergone the prerequisite fundamental social and economic changes. Outside Europe, gradual assimilation of the "new," which had characterized change and cultural diffusion for 5,000 years, had to be replaced by hurried imitation, which proved enormously disorienting. This combination of innovation and imitation produced an unprecedented and persisting imbalance among various parts of the Oikoumene. Muslims' responses paralleled those of other "non-Western" peoples but were often filtered through and expressed in peculiarly Islamic or Islamicate symbols and motifs. The power of Islam as a source of public values had already waxed and waned many times; it intensified in the 18th and 19th centuries, receded in the early 20th century, and surged again after the mid-20th century. Thus, European colonizers appeared in the midst of an ongoing process that they greatly affected but did not completely transform.

Precolonial Reform and Experimentation from 1683 to 1818

From the mid-17th century through the 18th and early 19th centuries, certain Muslims expressed an awareness of internal weakness in their societies. In some areas, Muslims were largely unaware of the rise of Europe; in others, such as India, Sumatra, and Java, the 18th century actually brought European control. Responses to decline, sometimes official and sometimes unofficial, sometimes Islamizing and sometimes Europeanizing, fell into two categories, as the following examples demonstrate.

In some areas leaders attempted to revive existing political systems. In Iran, for example, attempts at restoration combined military and religious reform. About 1730 a Turk from Khorāsān named Nadr Qolī Beg reorganized the Ṣafavid army in the name of the Ṣafavid shah, whom he replaced with himself in 1736. Taking the title Nādir Shah, he extended the borders of the Ṣafavid state farther than ever; he even defeated the Ottomans and may have aspired to be the leader of all Muslims. To this end he made overtures to neighbouring rulers, seeking their recognition by trying to represent Iranian Shīʿism as a

Nadir Shah, painting by an unknown artist, *c.* 1740; in the Victoria and Albert Museum, London.

madhhab (school of Islamic law) alongside the Sunni *madhhab*s. After he was killed in 1747, however, his reforms did not survive and his house disintegrated. Karīm Khan Zand, a general from Shīrāz, ruled in the name of the Ṣafavids but did not restore real power to the shah. By the time the Qājārs (1779–1925) managed to resecure Iran's borders, reviving Ṣafavid legitimacy was impossible.

In the Ottoman Empire restoration involved selective imitation of things European. Its first phase, from 1718 to 1730, is known as the Tulip Period because of the cultivation by the wealthy of a Perso-Turkish flower then popular in Europe. Experimentation with European manners and tastes was matched by experimentation with European military technology. Restoration depended on reinvigorating the military, the key to earlier Ottoman success, and Christian Europeans were hired for the task. After Nādir Shah's defeat of the Ottoman army, this first phase of absolutist restoration ended, but the pursuit of European fashion had become a permanent element in Ottoman life. Meanwhile, central power continued to weaken, especially in the area of international commerce. The certificates of protection that had accompanied the Capitulations arrangements for foreign nationals were extended to non-Muslim Ottoman subjects, who gradually oriented themselves toward their foreign associates. The integration of such groups into the Ottoman state was further weakened by the recognition, in the disastrous Treaty of Küçük Kaynarca (1774), of the Russian tsar as protector of the Ottoman's Greek Orthodox *millet*.

A second stage of absolutist restoration occurred under Selim III, who became sultan in the first year of the French Revolution and ruled until 1807. His military and political reforms, referred to as the "new order" (*nizam-ı cedid*), went beyond the Tulip Period in making use of things European; for example, the enlightened monarch, as exemplified by Napoleon himself, became an Ottoman ideal. There, as in Egypt under Muḥammad ʿAlī (reigned 1805–48), the famed corps of Janissaries, the elite troops that had been a source of Ottoman strength, was destroyed and replaced with European-trained troops.

In other areas, leaders envisioned or created new social orders that were self-consciously Islamic. The growing popularity of Westernization and a decreasing reliance on Islam as a source of public values was counterbalanced in many parts of Islamdom by all sorts of Islamic activism, ranging from educational reform to jihad. Islamic politics often were marked by an oppositional quality that drew on long-standing traditions of skepticism about government. Sufism could play very different roles. In the form of renovated *ṭarīqahs*, fellowships around particular Islamic masters, it could support reform and stimulate a consciousness marked by Pan-Islamism (the idea that Islam can be the basis of a unified political and cultural order). Sufis often encouraged the study of tales about the Prophet Muhammad (Hadith), which they used to establish him as a model for spiritual and moral reconstruction and to invalidate many unacceptable traditional or customary Islamic practices. Sufi *ṭarīqahs* provided interregional communication and contact and an indigenous form of social organization that in some cases led to the founding of a dynasty, as with the Libyan monarchy.

Sufism could also be condemned as a source of degeneracy. The most famous and influential militant anti-Sufi movement arose in the Arabian Peninsula and called itself al-Muwaḥḥidūn ("the Monotheists"), but it came to be known as Wahhābiyyah, after its founder, Muḥammad ibn ʿAbd al-Wahhāb (1703–92). Inspired by Ibn Taymiyyah (*see above* Migration and renewal [1041–1405]), Ibn al-Wahhāb argued that the Qurʾān and Sunnah could provide the basis for a reconstruction of Islamic society out of the degenerate form in which it had come to be practiced. Islam itself was not an inhibiting force; "traditional" Islam was. Far from advocating the traditional, the Wahhābīs argued that what had become traditional had strayed very far from the fundamental, which can always be found in the Qur᾽ān and Sunnah. The traditional they associated with blind imitation (*taqlīd*); reform, with making the pious personal effort (*ijtihād*) necessary to understand the fundamentals. Within an Islamic context this type of movement was not conservative, because it sought not to conserve what had been passed down but to renew what had been abandoned. The Wahhābī movement attracted the support of a tribe in the Najd led by Muḥammad ibn Saʿūd. Although the first state produced by this alliance did not last, it laid the foundations for the existing Saudi state in Arabia and inspired similar activism elsewhere down to the present day.

In West Africa a series of activist movements appeared from the 18th century into the 19th. There, as in Arabia, Islamic activism was directed less at non-Muslims than at Muslims who had gone astray. As in many of Islamdom's outlying areas, emergent groups of indigenous educated, observant Muslims, such as the Tukulor, were finding the casual, syncretistic, opportunistic nature of official Islam to be increasingly intolerable. Such Muslims were inspired by reformist scholars from numerous times and places—e.g., al-Ghazālī, al-Suyūṭī, and al-Maghīlī—and by a theory of jihad comparable to that of the Wahhābīs and by expectations of a *mujaddid* at the turn of the Islamic century in AH 1200 (1785 CE). In what is now northern Nigeria, the discontent of the 1780s and '90s erupted in 1804, when Usman dan Fodio declared a jihad against the Hausa rulers. Others followed, among them Muḥammad al-Jaylānī in Aïr, Shehuh Ahmadu Lobbo in Macina, al-Ḥājj ʿUmar Tal (a member of the reformist Tijānī *ṭarīqah*) in Fouta Djallon, and Samory in the Malinke (Mandingo) states. Jihad activity continued for a century; it again became millennial near the turn of the next Muslim century, in AH 1300 (1882 CE), as the need to resist European occupation became more urgent. For example, Muḥammad Aḥmad declared himself to be the Mahdī in the Sudan in 1881.

The Muslim reformer and military leader Samory engaged in jihad in the Malinke (Mandingo) state, resisting colonialism until his capture by French troops in 1898.

In the Indian Ocean area Islamic activism was more often intellectual and educational. Its best exemplar was Shāh Walī Allāh of Delhi (1702–62), the spiritual ancestor of many later Indian Muslim reform movements. During his lifetime the collapse of Muslim political power was painfully evident. He tried to unite the Muslims of India, not around Sufism as Akbar had tried to do but around the Sharīʿah. Like Ibn Taymiyyah, he understood the Sharīʿah to be based on firm sources—the Qurʾān and Sunnah—that could with pious effort be applied to present circumstances. Once again the study of Hadith provided a rich array of precedents and inspired a positive spirit of social reconstruction akin to that of the Prophet Muhammad.

THE RISE OF BRITISH COLONIALISM TO THE END OF THE OTTOMAN EMPIRE

The many efforts to revive and resist were largely unsuccessful. By 1818 British hegemony over India was complete, and many other colonies and mandates followed between then and the aftermath of World War I. Not all Muslim territories were colonized, but nearly all experienced some kind of dependency, be it psychological, political, technological, cultural, or economic. Perhaps only the Saudi regime in the central parts of the Arabian Peninsula could be said to have escaped any kind of dependency, but even there oil exploration, begun in the 1930s, brought European interference. In the 19th century Westernization and Islamic activism coexisted and competed. By the turn of the 20th century secular ethnic nationalism had become the most common mode of protest in Islamdom, but the spirit of Islamic reconstruction was also kept alive, either in conjunction with secular nationalism or in opposition to it.

In the 19th-century Ottoman Empire, selective Westernization coexisted with a reconsideration of Islam. The program of reform known as the Tanzimat, which was in effect from 1839 to 1876, aimed to emulate European law and administration by giving all Ottoman subjects equal legal standing regardless of religious confession and by limiting the powers of the monarch. In the 1860s a group known as the Young Ottomans tried to identify the basic principles of European liberalism—and even love of nation—with Islam itself. In Iran the Qājār shahs brought in a special "Cossack Brigade," trained and led by Russians, while at the same time the Shīʿite *mujtahids* viewed the decisions of their spiritual leader as binding on all Iranian Shīʿites and declared themselves to be independent of the shah. (One Shīʿite revolt, that of the Bāb [died 1850], led to a whole new religion, Bahāʾī.) Like the Young Ottomans, Shīʿite religious leaders came to identify with constitutionalism in opposition to the ruler.

As grand vizier of the Ottoman Empire, Mustafa Reşid Paşa took a leading part in initiating, drafting, and promulgating the first of the reform edicts known as the Tanzimat (“Reorganization”).

Islamic protest often took the form of jihads against Europeans: by Southeast Asians against the Dutch; by the Sanūsī *ṭarīqah* over Italian control in Libya; by the Mahdist movement in the Sudan; or by the Ṣaliḥī *ṭarīqah* in Somalia, led by Sayyid Muḥammad ibn ʿAbd Allāh Ḥasan, who was tellingly nicknamed the Mad Mullah by Europeans. Sometimes religious leaders, such as those of the Shīʿites in Iran (1905–11), took part in constitutional revolutions. Underlying much of this activity was a Pan-Islamic sentiment that drew on very old conceptions of the *ummah* (Muslim community) as the ultimate solidarity group for Muslims. Three of the most prominent Islamic reconstructionists were Jamāl al-Dīn al-Afghānī, his Egyptian disciple Muḥammad ʿAbduh, and the Indian poet Sir Muḥammad Iqbāl. All warned against the blind pursuit of Westernization, arguing that blame for the weaknesses of

YOUNG OTTOMANS AND YOUNG TURKS

The Young Ottomans (in Turkish, Yeni Osmanlilar) were a secret Turkish nationalist organization formed in Istanbul in June 1865 that favoured converting the Turkish-dominated multinational Ottoman Empire into a more purely Turkish state and called for the creation of a constitutional government. By 1867 the Young Ottomans had expanded from the original 6 members to 245, including the noted poets Namık Kemal and Ziya Paşa; they were further supported financially and materially by the Egyptian prince Mustafa Fazıl and had attracted the attention of the Ottoman princes Murad and Abdülhamid.

Exiled for revolutionary activities by the grand vizier Âli Paşa in 1867, the society established itself in Paris; there it made

continued on the next page

continued from the previous page

European contacts and began publishing *Hürriyet* ("Freedom"), an inflammatory newspaper, subsequently smuggled into Turkey, calling on the Turkish people to demand a constitution. The return to Istanbul of Mustafa Fazıl and Namık Kemal weakened the Young Ottomans, and in 1871–72, during the amnesty declared after the death of Âli Paşa, most of them returned to Turkey. The movement, however, had lost its impetus and, except for the isolated activity of such individuals as Namık Kemal, ceased to be a factor in national affairs.

The Young Ottomans were the forerunner of other Turkish nationalist groups, most notably the Young Turks (in Turkish, Jöntürkler). The Young Turks were the coalition of various reform groups that led a revolutionary movement against the authoritarian regime of Ottoman sultan Abdülhamid II in 1908, which culminated in the establishment of a constitutional government.

While in power, the Young Turks introduced programs that promoted the modernization of the Ottoman Empire and a new spirit of Turkish nationalism. They carried out administrative reforms, especially of provincial administration, that led to more centralization, and they were the first Ottoman reformers to promote industrialization. In addition, the programs of the Young Turk regime effectuated greater secularization of the legal system and provided for the education of women and better state-operated primary schools. Such positive developments in domestic affairs, however, were largely overshadowed by the disastrous consequences of the regime's foreign policy decisions that resulted in the dissolution of the Ottoman state. An overly hasty appraisal of Germany's military capability by the Young Turk leaders led them to break neutrality and enter World War I (1914–18) on the side of the Central Powers. Ottoman troops made an important contribution to the Central

Powers' war effort, fighting on multiple fronts. In 1915, members of the Young Turk government directed Ottoman soldiers and their proxies in Eastern Anatolia, near the Russian front, to deport or execute millions of Armenians in an event that later came to be known as the Armenian Genocide. Upon the end of the war, with defeat imminent, the cabinet resigned on October 9, 1918, less than a month before the Ottomans signed the Armistice of Mudros.

Muslims lay not with Islam but rather with Muslims themselves, because they had lost touch with the progressive spirit of social, moral, and intellectual reconstruction that had made early Islamicate civilization one of the greatest in human history.

Although al-Afghānī, who taught and preached in many parts of Islamdom, acknowledged that organization by nationality might be necessary, he viewed it as inferior to Muslim identity. He further argued that Western technology could advance Muslims only if they retained and cultivated their own spiritual and cultural heritage. He pointed out that at one time Muslims had been intellectual and scientific leaders in the world, identifying a golden age under the ʿAbbāsid caliphate and pointing to the many contributions Muslims had made to "the West." Like al-Afghānī, Iqbāl assumed that without Islam Muslims could never regain the strength they had possessed when they were a vital force in the world, united in a single international community and unaffected by differences of language or ethnos. This aggressive recovery of the past became a permanent theme of Islamic reconstruction. In many regions of Islamdom the movement known as Salafiyyah also identified with an ideal time in history, that of the "pious ancestors" (*salaf*) in the early

Muslim state of Muhammad and his companions, and advocated past-oriented change to bring present-day Muslims up to the progressive standards of an earlier ideal.

In addition to clearly Islamic thinkers, there were others, such as the Egyptian Muṣṭafā Kāmil, whose nationalism was not simply secular. Kāmil saw Egypt as simultaneously European, Ottoman, and Muslim. The Young Turk Revolution of 1908 was followed by a period in which similarly complex views of national identity were discussed in the Ottoman Empire.

Chapter 4

Revival and Globalization (The Early 20th Century to the Present)

The tension between Islamic and national identification remained crucial for Muslims at the start of the 20th century. In countries under Western colonial rule, the struggle for national independence often went hand in hand with an effort by reformist intellectuals to recover what they thought was the authentic message of the original Muslim community. Between the two World Wars, two distinct interpretations of Islam emerged from the Salafiyyah movement.

One interpretation, drawing upon Pan-Islamism, politicized Islam by taking its scriptures to be the proper foundation of the social and political order. The writings of the Syrian Egyptian scholar Rashīd Riḍā (1865–1935) provided a basis for such an interpretation. Like earlier reformers, Riḍā viewed the cult of saints (the veneration of holy figures) as a corruption of Islam, and he sought a renovated religion that would be grounded in and faithful to the early scriptures. He insisted, moreover, that such a renovation entailed the implementation of Islamic precepts in social and political life. Riḍā considered the 1924 dissolution of the Ottoman caliphate to be a traumatic event, because the Muslim community thereby lost its major religious and political representative. He also hailed the seizure of Mecca by the Arabian tribal leader ʿAbd al-ʿAziz ibn Saʿūd that same year. This led to the founding in 1932 of the modern state of Saudi Arabia, which Riḍā considered a model Islamic state.

The politicized interpretation of Islam envisioned by Rashīd Riḍā influenced such thinkers as Ḥasan al-Bannā, founder of the Muslim Brotherhood, an influential militant organization.

Riḍā was quite influential among Muslims who were hoping for a wholly Islamic society. For example, his thought inspired Ḥasan al-Bannā (1906–49), who in Egypt in 1928 founded the militant organization the Muslim Brotherhood. The Brotherhood later influenced other militant Islamic groups.

In contrast to these thinkers, the Egyptian reformer ʿAlī ʿAbd al-Rāziq (1888–1966) claimed that Islam could not be the basis of a society's political system. After direct revelation from God ended with Muhammad, al-Rāziq maintained, Islam could have only a spiritual function; the use of the religion for political aims could not be legitimate. The caliphate was merely a political construction and not an essential aspect of Islam. Its disappearance with the end of the Ottoman Empire, therefore, was not a matter of concern. Henceforward, each predominantly Muslim country would be free to determine its own political system. Although the great majority of the ulama rejected ʿAbd al-Rāziq's view, secular elites blended it with a liberal conception of society that regarded religion as only one of several cultural elements rather than as a comprehensive code of life. In Egypt, for example, liberal intellectuals such as Ṭāhā Ḥusayn (1889–1973) viewed their national culture as incorporating Islamic, Arab, ancient Egyptian, and European elements.

The question of whether Islam should be the foundation of a national culture and politics dominated political discourse in Islamic countries throughout the 20th century and beyond. In particular, the political interpretation of Islam emerged alongside resistance to Western acculturation. Religious scholars and intellectuals such as ʿAbd al-Hamid ibn Badis (1899–1940), founder in 1931 of the Association of Algerian Muslim Ulama, and ʿAllāl al-Fāsī (1910–74) in Morocco reconceived the identity of their countries in Islamic terms and played significant roles in nationalist movements until independence was achieved. Between the two World Wars, these scholars established several Islamic private schools offering Arabic-language instruction for boys and girls. Islamic intellectuals and movements often put their educational endeavours at the centre of their projects to bring Islam into agreement with their times. Thus, the question of the transmission of Islamic knowledge versus secular and Westernized education became crucial. Many Islamic thinkers viewed the two systems of education as compatible, arguing that they should be integrated and could complement each other. The Indonesian Nahdatul Ulama, for instance, favoured a system of Islamic schooling along modernized lines that would integrate religious and secular knowledge.

POSTCOLONIAL STATES AND ISLAM

Later in the 20th century, colonized Muslim societies (except Palestine) gradually achieved political independence and built new states. Many of these states adopted a "Muslim" identity that they interpreted in various ways and implemented within such domains as law, education, and moral conduct. Two states, though established in societies that had not been colonized, exemplified contrasting paradigms. In 1924 the Turkish military officer Mustafa Kemal, taking the name Atatürk ("Father of the Turks"), brought a formal end to the Ottoman caliphate. Maintaining that Islam had contributed to the backwardness of Turkish society and that a modern country must be founded upon science and reason rather than religion, Atatürk claimed to relegate Islam to the private sphere. This brand of secularist government also controlled the public expression of Islam and did not separate state and religion. In Saudi Arabia, on the other hand, the state regulated public life according to Islamic norms, using a rigorous interpretation of Sharīʿah (Islamic law).

In Egypt, which became a constitutional monarchy after 1922 (though it was under colonial control until 1952),

Mustafa Kemal Atatürk.

the question of the relation between state and Islam generated fierce political controversies between secularists and those who interpreted Islam as a system of government. Among the latter, the Muslim Brotherhood grew from a grassroots organization into a mass movement that provided key popular support for the 1952 Revolution of the Free Officers, a military coup led by Col. Gamal Abdel Nasser that ousted the monarchy. Similar movements in Palestine, Syria, Jordan, and North Africa, the politicized heirs of earlier reformist intellectual trends, later emerged as significant actors in their respective political scenes. It was not until the end of the 1960s, however, that they became strong enough to pose a serious political challenge to their countries' authoritarian regimes.

Islamist Movements from the 1960s

With the defeat in June 1967 of the Arab states by Israel in the Six-Day (June) War, socialist and Pan-Arab ideologies declined in the Islamic world, while political Islam emerged as a public force. Egypt, which had been under the influence of the Soviet Union since the mid-1950s, withdrew from military and other treaties with the Soviets in the 1970s under Pres. Anwar el-Sādāt. A new alliance between Egypt and Saudi Arabia, fostered by economic assistance to Egypt from Saudi Arabia and other oil-producing Persian Gulf states, altered the geopolitical map of Islam and led to new religious dynamics. In 1962 the Saudi regime established the Muslim World League in Mecca with the participation of Muslim scholars and intellectuals from all over the world. The league, whose mission was to unify Muslims and promote the spread of Islam, opened offices in the Islamic world in the 1960s and in the West in subsequent decades. With financial assistance as well as religious guidance from the league, new Islamic organizations were created by revivalist movements in the Islamic world and by immigrant Muslim communities in Europe and America.

During this period Islamist movements that insisted that society and government should conform to Islamic values began to openly criticize state control of Islam in their countries and condemned their governments' minimalist interpretations of Islamic norms. These movements were diverse from the start and did not reach public prominence until 1979, when an Islamic state was founded in Iran through revolution.

The Iranian Revolution was influenced by Third Worldism (a political ideology emphasizing the economic gap between developed Western states and countries in other parts of the world) and by Marxism; particularly important were the vehement critique of Western influence developed by Jalāl Al-e-Ahmed (1923–69) and the Marxist-oriented Islamic reformism promoted by ʿAlī Sharīʿatī (1933–77). The revolution's leader, Ayatollah Ruhollah Khomeini (1900–89), emphasized the themes of defending the disinherited (referred to by the Qurʾānic word *mustadhʿafin*) and resisting "Westoxification" (Farsi: *gharbzadegī*), a concept he borrowed from Al-e-Ahmed

As leader of the Iranian Revolution, Ayatollah Ruhollah Khomeini launched a strong critique of the Western world, promoting a Marxist-influenced Islamic ideology.

and Sharīʿatī. He also coined and implemented in the new Islamic republic the concept of *velāyat-e faqīh*, or government by the Muslim jurist. The Iranian Revolution gave hope to many Islamist movements with similar programs by demonstrating the potential of Islam as a foundation for political mobilization and resistance. It further provided them with a blueprint for political action against governments that they believed had betrayed authentic Islam and grown corrupt and authoritarian. The Islamic republic of Iran also competed with Saudi Arabia at the international level for influence in the Middle East.

Even before the Iranian Revolution, however, offshoots of the Muslim Brotherhood were radicalizing political Islam in other parts of the Islamic world. One of the most important figures in this trend was the Egyptian author and Muslim Brotherhood member Sayyid Quṭb. Quṭb, a prolific writer, was executed by the Nasser regime in 1966 but remained an influential voice among Islamists after his death. In his prison writings Quṭb declared that the influence of Western-inspired secularism had caused his society to become un-Islamic and that a new vanguard of Muslims must bring it back to Islam; he saw this as the "solution" to the two failed secular ideologies, capitalism and communism, that had relegated religion to the periphery of government throughout the Islamic world. Thus, a new *ummah* under the sole sovereignty of Allāh and his revealed word needed to be constituted, because secular nation-states—exemplified by Nasserist Egypt—had led only to barbarity. Quṭb's ideology was also influenced by Abū al-Aʿlā al-Mawdūdī (1903–79), founder in British India in 1941 of the Islamic Assembly, the first Islamic political party. The Islamic Assembly was reconfigured after the partition of Pakistan and India in 1947 in order to support the establishment of an Islamic state in Pakistan.

Beginning in the 1970s, a new generation of political activists who used violence and had no thorough Islamic education declared that their national leaders were "apostates" who had to be eliminated

THE MUSLIM BROTHERHOOD

The Muslim Brotherhood (in Arabic, al-Ikhwān al-Muslimūn) is a religio-political organization founded in 1928 at Ismailia, Egypt, by Ḥasan al-Bannāʾ. It advocated a return to the Qurʾān and the Hadith as guidelines for a healthy modern Islamic society. The Brotherhood spread rapidly throughout Egypt, Sudan, Syria, Palestine, Lebanon, and North Africa. Although figures of Brotherhood membership are variable, it is estimated that at its height in the late 1940s it may have had some 500,000 members.

Initially centred on religious and educational programs, the Muslim Brotherhood was seen as providing much-needed social services, and in the 1930s its membership grew swiftly. In the late 1930s the Brotherhood began to politicize its outlook, and, as an opponent of Egypt's ruling Wafd party, during World War II it organized popular protests against the government.

With the advent of the revolutionary regime in Egypt in 1952, the Brotherhood retreated underground. An attempt to assassinate Egyptian Pres. Gamal Abdel Nasser in Alexandria on October 26, 1954, led to the Muslim Brotherhood's forcible suppression. In the 1960s and '70s the Brotherhood's activities remained largely clandestine.

In the 1980s the Muslim Brotherhood experienced a renewal as part of the general upsurge of religious activity in Islamic countries. The Brotherhood's new adherents aimed to reorganize society and government according to Islamic doctrines, and they were vehemently anti-Western. An uprising by the Brotherhood in the Syrian city of Ḥamāh in February 1982 was crushed by the government of Ḥafiz al-Assad at a cost of perhaps 25,000 lives. The Brotherhood revived in Egypt and Jordan in the same period, and, beginning in the late 1980s, it emerged to compete in legislative elections in those countries.

In Egypt, the participation of the Muslim Brotherhood

continued on the next page

continued from the previous page

n parliamentary elections in the 1980s was followed by the Brotherhood's boycott of the elections of 1990, when it joined most of the country's opposition in protesting electoral strictures. Although the group itself remained formally banned, in the 2000 elections Brotherhood supporters running as independent candidates were able to win 17 seats, making it the largest opposition bloc in the parliament.

In January 2011 a nonreligious youth protest movement against the Ḥosnī Mubārak regime appeared in Egypt. After hesitating briefly, the Muslim Brotherhood's senior leadership endorsed the movement and called on its members to participate in demonstrations. The protests soon forced Mubārak to step down as president in February, clearing the way for the Muslim Brotherhood's open participation in Egyptian politics.

In late April 2011 the Muslim Brotherhood founded a political party called the Freedom and Justice Party and applied for official recognition from the Egyptian interim government. Leaders of the Freedom and Justice Party stated that the party's policies would be grounded in Islamic principles but that the party, whose members included women and Christians, would be nonconfessional. The party received official recognition in June, allowing it to enter candidates in upcoming elections. The Freedom and Justice Party soon achieved considerable success, winning about 47 percent of seats in elections held between November 2011 and January 2012 for the People's Assembly, the lower house of the Egyptian parliament.

Mohammed Morsi, the head of the Freedom and Justice Party, won the presidential election held in May and June 2012. His administration faced increasingly vocal opposition in 2013, led by activists who accused the incumbents of inaction regarding Egypt's weak economy, failing public services, and deteriorating security situation. A massive protest calling for Morsi's resignation was held on June 30, 2013, the first anniversary of his inauguration. On

July 3 the military suspended the constitution, removed Morsi from the presidency, and appointed a new transitional administration. Morsi and several other Muslim Brotherhood figures were placed under arrest, and television stations associated with the Muslim Brotherhood were shut down.

While Morsi's opponents celebrated, enraged supporters of the Muslim Brotherhood took to the streets to denounce the removal of a democratically elected leader. Violence escalated on August 14 when Egyptian security forces launched raids to clear Muslim Brotherhood sit-ins in Cairo, killing more than 1,000 over a period of several days. The attacks were accompanied by sweeping arrests of Muslim Brotherhood leaders and suspected members. In September 2013 a Cairo court formally restored the Mubārak-era ban on the Muslim Brotherhood, freezing the activities of the group and all its affiliated organizations.

by force. In 1981 the radical group Egyptian Islamic Jihad assassinated Egyptian Pres. Anwar el-Sādāt for the 1979 peace treaty he had made with Israel, among other things. This trend was also present in North Africa and South Asia. In many cases these activists were violently repressed. In some instances conflicts with government authorities led to bloody civil wars, as in Algeria between 1992 and 2002, or to protracted armed struggles between military forces and Islamist groups, as in Egypt from the 1970s to the mid-1990s. This repression resulted in the exile of many Islamist activists to Europe and the Americas and led many others to join such military fronts as the Afghan Jihad.

The Mainstreaming of Islamist Movements

From the late 1970s, Islamist groups were the object of sustained worldwide media attention. Yet nonviolent groups received significantly less attention than the few groups that advocated the use of violence. Nonviolent Islamists often expressed their willingness to participate in legal electoral politics. This became possible in the 1990s, when authoritarian regimes—faced with serious socioeconomic crises and seeking to legitimize themselves in the eyes of the public—implemented policies of limited political liberalization.

The Muslim Brotherhood first engaged in electoral politics in Egypt in the 1980s and in Jordan as early as 1989. In Morocco the Party of Justice and Development elected its first parliamentary representatives in 1997. In Indonesia the Prosperous Justice Party took part in legislative elections in 2004. Turkey allowed Islamists not only to participate in elections but also to govern at the national level. In 2002 Recep Tayyip Erdoğan, chairman of the Party of Justice and Development, which won a majority of seats in that year's general

Recep Tayyip Erdoğan, an Islamist, served as prime minister of Turkey from 2003 until 2014, at which point he assumed the presidency.

elections, formed a pragmatic Islamist government that cultivated diplomatic relations with Western powers.

In all these cases, mainstream opposition Islamist movements demonstrated their power to mobilize voters, a consequence of their social and charitable activism, their programs of good governance, and their fight against government corruption. Despite their tendencies to speak about the universality of the Muslim community, mainstream Islamists remained nationalistic. Holding a conservative view of politics, they abandoned the revolutionary and utopian aspects of radical activism and instead struggled to moralize public and political life—e.g., by protesting "indecent" forms of entertainment and public behaviour and by insisting on accountability for political authorities. When they were allowed to govern, they rarely imposed Sharīʿah-based legislation. Laws inspired by the Islamic legal tradition were implemented, however, in various forms in Iran after the 1979 revolution and in northern Sudan after 1983.

In countries that did not practice electoral politics, movements of opposition devised other means of protest and participation. In Saudi Arabia in 1992 a "Memorandum of Advice" was signed by more than 100 ulama and Islamists and was sent to Sheikh ʿAbd al-ʿAzīz ibn Bāz, the head of the Board of Senior Ulama and grand mufti of the state, to be passed on to the king. They requested an even greater role for the ulama, a comprehensive implementation of Sharīʿah in Saudi society, social welfare programs, respect for human rights, and a reorientation of Saudi foreign policy along "Islamic" lines.

Contemporary Islamist movements are polarized between two main trends. On the one hand, most movements are mainstream and pragmatic, seeking eventually to govern through participation in the political system and public debate. On the other hand, more-radical opposition groups reject electoral politics and seek revolutionary change, sometimes violently. Some groups alternate between these poles, choosing electoral participation or violence depending upon political circumstances, as in the case of Ḥamāsin the West Bank and Gaza Strip and Hezbollah in Lebanon. Beginning in the last decade of the 20th century, some groups disconnected themselves from national politics in order to join transnational movements.

DIMENSIONS OF THE ISLAMIC REVIVAL

Various scholars have argued that Islamist movements emerged in reaction to the failure of state-led modernization projects and to general socioeconomic problems such as youth unemployment and poverty. Yet Islamist movements are not limited to poor countries or to disadvantaged, marginalized groups. In fact, members of these

Supporters of Hezbollah wave their party flag alongside the national flag of Lebanon during a commemoration in the town of Bint Jbeil, Lebanon, on August 13, 2016.

movements are generally highly educated, predominantly in secular fields, as a result of state-led modernization projects. In particular, mainstream Islamist parties are typically led by young men and women who are successful professionals with college or university degrees.

Scholars also have attempted to explain Islamism's rise as the direct result of the failure of Pan-Arabism in the Arab Middle East and of secular nationalism in the Islamic world. As their Arab or national self-identifications break down, according to this view, people living in those countries turn to Islamism as a replacement. This is a misconception for two reasons. First, earlier forms of nationalism in Islamic countries were not devoid of religious ideas. Second, state institutions in those countries regulated and influenced the legal and public manifestations of Islam, in particular through their systems of public education.

In addition to becoming politicized in the hands of opposition movements and governments in the second half of the 20th century, Islam also followed a dynamic of revival that was deeply linked to sweeping educational, demographic, and social transformations. A young generation came of age in the 1960s, a time of rural exodus and urbanization, without having experienced colonial times. General access to education and the availability of printed Islamic literature also gave these young people an opportunity to build their own interpretations of Islam. Muslims could now study the Qurʾān and the Sunnah without the mediation of the ulama, who represented a more institutionalized interpretation of Islam.

Technological innovations allowed some Islamic preachers to be heard or read, and even to develop followings, across the world. In the 1970s both the Ayatollah Khomeini and the Egyptian preacher Sheikh Kishk disseminated their speeches and sermons on audiocassettes. In the 1990s such new media as satellite television and the Internet began to offer faster means of access to ideas about Islam. In the late 1990s the Egyptian ʿAmr Khālid became one of many popular preachers who reached a global audience. Through his website he disseminated advice on understanding and living Islam as a general ethics and on specific disciplines for achieving success and happiness in this world and in the afterlife.

Social change in the Islamic world also encouraged Muslims to reevaluate gender relations. As Muslim women gained significant access to higher education and the job market, they became integral to public life in Muslim countries. In many instances, they sought to express their piety in the public sphere by drawing from and adapting Islamic tradition. One of the most widespread and (since the late 20th century) controversial expressions of piety among Muslim women was hijab, or the wearing of the veil. Veiling was never a uniform practice: elite women of earlier generations had unveiled, and the veils themselves ranged from a simple scarf to a full-body covering, depending upon country, culture, and economic class. In some Muslim countries—notably Iran and Saudi Arabia—veiling was required by law. Yet in many other countries and in the Muslim minority communities of Europe, Australia, and the United States,

Since the late 20th century, the wearing of the veil by Muslim women has been much debated throughout the Islamic world. Some countries have tried to limit the use of headscarves while others have sought to make it obligatory.

veiling was a massive voluntary phenomenon beginning in the 1970s. The veil remains a subject of political and religious controversy in Western countries with large Muslim minorities and throughout the Islamic world.

Islam and Globalization: The Age of Mobility

Emigration of Muslims from the Middle East and South Asia accelerated after World War II and eventually produced large Muslim communities in the United States, Canada, and the countries of western Europe. While Islam was becoming politicized in the Islamic world, Western Muslims pondered how they could live and practice their religion in a non-Muslim context and whether full participation in Western culture and political life was possible, let alone desirable. These issues prompted the formation of numerous Muslim religious and cultural organizations in the West in the 1980s and '90s, including the Islamic Society of North America, the Union of Islamic Organizations in France, and the European Council for Fatwa and Research. These groups attempted to provide guidance to Muslims who wished to preserve their Islamic identity while contributing to the political and social life of their adoptive countries.

In the first and second decade of the 21st century, Western Muslims were still not fully integrated into their societies, and many suffered various forms of discrimination. Many also retained important links with their countries of origin through frequent travel and modern means of communication (e.g., the Internet). Second- and third-generation immigrants often had the opportunity to redefine Islamic practices and beliefs in opposition to their parents and grandparents, whose interpretations they considered too parochial, too strongly influenced by the culture of origin, or not close enough to a more abstract and universal type of Islam. While thus articulating a more personal religious identity, young Western Muslims (like young Muslims in other parts of the world) came to rely on self-proclaimed religious authorities who were not associated with traditional institutions of Islamic learning. For this young generation, the fatwas (formal opinions on questions of Islamic doctrine) issued by such authorities became a crucially important source of answers to political and ethical questions. These fatwas, moreover, tended to represent Islam as a moral rather than a political community.

It was in this context of the Western institutionalization of Islam, and more generally of the transformation of Islam from a blueprint for a political and legal system into an ethics of conduct, that the September 11, 2001, attacks against the United States occurred. The attacks were staged by al-Qaeda, a radical transnational Islamist

In the 21st century Western Muslims often have faced discrimination from other social groups over perceived cultural differences.

organization founded in the late 1980s by Osama bin Laden, a Saudi national. Bin Laden viewed the world as divided in a war between Muslims and "Crusaders and Zionists." Although the so-called "clash of civilizations" between Islam and the West was largely a theoretical construct, the term itself (popularized from 1993 by the political scientist Samuel P. Huntington) had a tremendously real power to mobilize public perceptions. The notion was reinforced both in the West and in the Islamic world by the September 11 attacks and the U.S.-led invasion of Afghanistan in 2001, the Iraq War in 2003, and the protracted inability of the international community to solve the conflict between the Palestinians and Israel.

The Islamic State in Syria and the Levant (ISIL), a transnational Sunni insurgent group, has its origins in the Iraq War of 2003–11. The group launched an offensive in early 2014 that drove Iraqi government forces out of key western cities, while in Syria it fought both government forces and rebel factions in the Syrian Civil War. In June 2014, after making significant territorial gains in Iraq, the group proclaimed the establishment of a caliphate led by the leader of ISIL, Abu Bakr al-Baghdadi.

ISIL's quick advances in Iraq alarmed the international community and set off a political crisis in Baghdad that ultimately led to the toppling of the Iraqi president. Calls for international intervention increased amid reports of extreme violence—public executions, displays of executed corpses, amputations, and lashings—as well as forced marriages and sex slavery. In September 2014 the United States, leading an international coalition that included Jordan, the United Arab Emirates, Bahrain, and Saudi Arabia, expanded its air campaign to include targets in Syria.

By mid-2015 ISIL appeared to be wearing down under the strain of its simultaneous confrontations with Kurdish forces and their Western allies, pro-Assad Syrian forces, and Iraqi forces. Faced

Members of ISIL parade through the Syrian city of Al-Raqqah on June 30, 2014.

with setbacks in its core territories, ISIL refocused its efforts on using international networks of militants to carry out attacks around the world. Through its online presence, ISIL has both recruited members and incited fear in non-Islamic nationals through video and images of violence perpetuated by the group. This new phase in ISIL's evolution was marked in November 2015 by its two bloodiest attacks to date outside of Iraq and Syria: on November 12 two suicide bombers struck a Shīʿite neighbourhood in Beirut, killing more than 40 people in retaliation for the Shīʿite militant group Hezbollah's intervention against ISIL in Syria; and a day later eight ISIL-affiliated gunmen launched a series of coordinated gun and bomb attacks in Paris, killing 129 people at several sites around the city. ISIL spokesmen claimed the attacks as revenge for France's participation in the international military campaign against ISIL.

Over the months that followed, a series of ISIL-linked attacks unfolded in North America, Asia, and Europe. In some cases, such as the bombing in March 2016 that killed 32 people at Brussels Airport, investigators were able to confirm that there had been operational coordination between the perpetrators and ISIL commanders. In other instances, though, such as two shooting rampages in the United States—in San Bernardino, California, in November 2015 and in Orlando, Florida, in June 2016—the perpetrators declared allegiance to ISIL but appeared not to have been in contact with its command structure. Such attacks, often called "homegrown" or "lone-wolf" attacks in the media, had been explicitly encouraged by ISIL in its propaganda as a way to spread violence beyond the reach of its networks of militants.

Boko Haram (in Hausa, "Westernization Is Sacrilege") was another Islamic sectarian movement whose violent acts caused concern around the world in the second decade of the 21st century. It was founded in 2002 by Mohammed Yusuf in northeastern Nigeria and since 2009 has carried out assassinations and large-scale acts of violence in that country. The group's initial proclaimed intent was to uproot the corruption and injustice in Nigeria, which it blamed on Western influences, and to impose Sharīʿah. In particular, Boko Haram drew worldwide condemnation after it perpetrated a mass kidnapping of more than 275 girls from a boarding school in Chibok in Borno state in April 2014, which generated an increase in offers of international assistance to Nigeria as the country attempted to quell Boko Haram's acts of terror. In March 2015 the group pledged allegiance to ISIL.

CONCLUSION

The Western civilizations of the world today are experiencing a resurgence of Islamophobia. Some of this fear is undoubtedly caused by the brutal actions of ISIL and similar groups. Yet it is important to remember that the religion of Islam is neither synonymous with the Islamic world nor with militant jihadist groups. The Islamic world does not exist in a vacuum; political action and religious warfare arise in response to global positioning of power. Amid the ubiquitous language of global religious warfare, there were internal debates between Muslims about how the religious tradition should be interpreted, particularly as it concerned the use of violence, women's rights, and interfaith relations. Intellectuals such as Nurcholis Majid in Indonesia and Amina Wadud in the United States attempted to reclaim Islamic traditions by showing how Islam could accommodate liberal-democratic societies and ideas. Their visions of Islam also recognized full gender equality and individual freedom of expression. Meanwhile, such controversies as the banning of the veil in public schools in France and the publication in Denmark of cartoons caricaturing the Islamic faith (and particularly the Prophet Muhammad) became instantly global, transforming intellectual and political debates between Islam and other faiths and within Islam itself and challenging the modes of regulation of Islam in Muslim and non-Muslim countries alike. The present and future state of the Islamic world appears to be a tumultuous one that can have lasting effects on both the state of the Islamic world and other civilizations.

GLOSSARY

ANTHROPOMORPHISM An interpretation of what is not human or personal in terms of human or personal characteristics.

CALIPHATE The office, term, or dominion of a caliph (a successor of Muhammad as temporal and spiritual head of Islam—used as a title).

CENTRIPETAL Proceeding or acting in a direction toward a centre.

EMIR A nobleman, independent chieftain, or native ruler especially in Arabia and Africa—used as a title.

FALSAFAH The Arabic cognate for the Greek philosophia, including metaphysics and logic, as well as the positive sciences, such as mathematics, music, astronomy, and anatomy.

HAJJ The pilgrimage to Mecca prescribed as a religious duty for Muslims.

HEGEMONY Influence or control over another country, a group of people, etc.

ISLAMDOM Of or relating to the complex of societies in which Muslims and their faith have been prevalent and socially dominant.

ISLAMIC Of or relating to Islam as a religion.

ISLAMICATE Of or relating to the social and cultural complex that is historically associated with Islam and Muslims, even when found among non-Muslims.

JIHAD Holy war waged on behalf of Islam as a religious duty.

OLIGARCHY A country, business, etc., that is controlled by a small group of people.

PAGAN A follower of a polytheistic religion.

PASTORALIST Of or relating to a social organization based on livestock raising as the primary economic activity.

PILGRIMAGE A journey to a holy place.

SEDENTARY Staying in one or the same place; not migratory.

SHARI'AH The body of formally established sacred law in Islam based primarily on God's commandments found in the Qurʾān and revealed through the sunna of Muhammad, governing in theory not only religious matters but regulating as well political, economic, civil, criminal, ethical, social, and domestic affairs in Muslim countries, and commonly in practice being supplemented by the customary law of a region.

SUFISM Ascetic Islamic mysticism originating in the 8th century and developing especially in Persia into a system of elaborate symbolism of which the goal is communion with the deity through contemplation and ecstasy.

ṬARĪQAH The Sufi path of spiritual development involving stages of meditation and contemplation leading to intimate communion with the deity.

ULAMA A group of Muslim theologians and scholars who are professionally occupied with the elaboration and interpretation of the Muslim legal system from a study of its sources in the Qurʾān and Hadith. They function individually as teachers, jurisconsults, and theologians, and constitute the highest body of religious authorities in Islam.

VIZIER A high executive officer of various Muslim countries.

BIBLIOGRAPHY

Surveys

The most visionary general work on Islamic history is Marshall G. S. Hodgson, *The Venture of Islam: Conscience and History in a World Civilization*, 3 vol. (1974), which sets Islam into a world historical context. A similar but shorter work, sumptuously illustrated, is Francis Robinson, *Atlas of the Islamic World Since 1500* (1982).

Regions of Islamdom

Peter B. Clarke, *West Africa and Islam: A Study of Religious Development from the 8th to the 20th Centuries* (1982); Jamil M. Abun-Nasr, *A History of the Maghrib*, 2nd ed. (1975); Clifford Geertz, *Islam Observed: Religious Development in Morocco and Indonesia* (1968, reissued 1971); S. M. Ikram, *Muslim Rule in India and Pakistan, 711–1858 A.C.*, rev. ed. (1966); Raphael Israeli, *Muslims in China: A Study in Cultural Confrontation* (1980); and Nehemia Levtzion (ed.), *Conversion to Islam* (1979).

Periods and Aspects of Islamicate History

Hamilton A. R. Gibb, *Studies on the Civilization of Islam* (1962, reissued 1982), is a collection of interpretive articles on history, historiography, literature, and philology. René Grousset, *The Empire of the Steppes: A History of Central Asia* (1970; originally published in French, 1939); and John J. Saunders, *The History of the Mongol Conquests* (1971), deal with the Mongol conquests. John J. Saunders (ed.), *The Muslim World on the Eve of Europe's Expansion* (1966), combines primary sources on the last three great Islamic empires; John Obert Voll, *Islam, Continuity and Change in the Modern World* (1982), provides an especially fine treatment of the 18th century; and Albert Hourani, *Arabic Thought in the Liberal Age*, 1798–1939 (1962), covers intellectual trends in the Arab Middle East in the first part of the 20th century.

Lois Beck and Nikki Keddie (eds.), *Women in the Muslim World* (1978); Elizabeth Warnock Fernea and Basima Qattan Bezirgan (eds.), *Middle Eastern Muslim Women Speak* (1977, reprinted 1984); and Jane I. Smith (ed.), *Women in Contemporary Muslim Societies* (1980), provide excellent studies of women in Islamic societies. A sociological analysis of developments among Islamic movements since the middle of the 20th century is Olivier Roy, *The Failure of Political Islam* (1994). Dale Eickelman and James Piscatori, *Muslim Politics* (1996), examines Islam's sociological, political, and intellectual transformations in the 20th century. John Esposito and John Voll, *Makers of Political Islam* (2001), is a study of the thought and life of crucial Muslim thinkers and activists in modern times. Peter Mandaville, *Transnational Muslim Politics: Reimagining the Umma* (2001), is an important overview of the effects of globalization and migrations on Islam and Muslims; and Giles Kepel, *Jihad: The Trail of Political Islam* (2002), analyzes the evolution of political Islam in the second half of the 20th century.

COLLECTIONS OF PRIMARY SOURCES IN ENGLISH TRANSLATION

Eric Schroeder, *Muhammad's People* (1955); Arthur Jeffery (ed.), *A Reader of Islam* (1962, reprinted 1980); John Alden Williams (ed.), *Islam* (1961, reissued 1967), and *Themes of Islamic Civilization* (1971, reprinted 1982); William H. McNeill and Marilyn Robinson Waldman, *The Islamic World* (1973, reprinted 1983); James Kritzeck, *Anthology of Islamic Literature* (1964, reissued 1975); and Bernard Lewis (ed.), *Islam: From the Prophet Muhammad to the Capture of Constantinople*, 2 vol. (1974, reissued 1976).

MAJOR REFERENCE WORKS

The Encyclopaedia of Islam, 5 vol. (1913–36), and a new edition, of which 5 vol. appeared from 1960 to 1986; *The Shorter Encyclopaedia of Islam* (1953, reprinted 1974), with articles culled from the *Encyclopaedia of Islam; The Cambridge History of Islam*, 2 vol. (1970, reprinted in 4 vol., 1980); Jean Sauvaget, *Jean Sauvaget's Introduction to the History of the Muslim East: A Bibliographical Guide* (1965, reprinted 1982; originally published in French, 2nd ed., 1961), a dated but still useful annotated bibliographic guide; Clifford Edmund Bosworth, *The Islamic Dynasties: A Chronological and Genealogical Handbook*, rev. ed. (1980); and *Encyclopedia of Women and Islamic Cultures*, 6 vol. (2003, 2005–07). Jean Jacques Waardenburg, *L'Islam dans le miroir de l'Occident*, 3rd rev. ed. (1970); and Edward W. Said, *Orientalism* (1978, reissued 1979), are critiques of Western approaches to Islam.

INDEX